First published in March 2000 by **GUILDHALL PRESS**

GUILDHALL PRESS is an imprint of
GP MEDIA
Unit 4, Community Service Units
Bligh's Lane, Derry BT48 0LZ
T: (02871) 364413
F: (02871) 372949
info@ghpress.freeserve.co.uk
www.ghpress.freeserve.co.uk

ISBN 0 946451 54 0

Printed in Ireland by Techman Ltd, Dublin

GP Media/Guildhall Press receives financial support from the District Partnership for the Derry City Council Area under the European Special Support Programme for Peace and Reconciliation and from the Londonderry Development Office under the Londonderry Regeneration Initiative. We would also like to thank Derry City Council's Recreation and Leisure Department for generous Community Services Grant Aid.

Before the Bandits

Shane White

GUILDHALL PRESS

Chapter One

"No, Winnie, no." My father's last words as my mother swerved to avoid the car ramming into them.

In a few moments he lay dead, the black umbrella he had used to defend himself lying by his side. The gunman smiled at my mother as he jumped into the revving car.

They say your life flashes in front of you when you die. I hope my father remembered the times we had in South Armagh, for it was here he was happiest. Here, where he felt among his own. An RUC Sergeant in a friendly welcoming area full of ordinary decent people. Nobody, but nobody, could have envisaged the day they would come for 'The Sergeant'. It wasn't always like that.

Let me take you back to 1961 when we first arrived in Forkhill, a village joining hands with Jonesborough, Silverbridge and Mullaghbawn on the edge of the glory of Slieve Gullion. A blue sky lightly dusted with cloud greeted our arrival as we pulled alongside and stopped at a row of white-washed terraced houses, elevated from the road and towering over the neglected Forester's Hall and the old farmhouse nestling opposite. This was the heart of South Armagh and my home for the next ten years. It is here my mind rests among the trailing beauty of its vivid countryside when I now think of home, despite leaving it some twenty eight years ago.

In just over a decade the media would daub this area 'Bandit Country'. An area whose beauty, in my opinion, is unrivalled throughout Ireland, with its stretching loughs, majestic heather clad mountains and its proud ancient churches.

5

My father, an RUC constable serving in Belfast, had been promoted and offered this outpost, a 'bog station' as it was known in the ranks. Advancement in the RUC didn't exactly nose dive here but it certainly didn't offer any long term promotional chances. My father was not really interested in a career, not from the point of view that going up the ladder was his sole aim; no, that was being a good honest policeman and having a bit of crack in the meantime. I don't recall whether he was overjoyed or not with his promotion. I noticed little variance in my sweet ration nor the whacks across my legs. This was how a six year old gauged life. Life seemed more or less normal, the only difference being our lives were now located elsewhere.

Sitting outside our house in the Andersonstown district of Belfast my brother and I sat patiently in the car waiting for our parents and our grandmother. A packet of Tayto crisps and a bar of toffee stared up at us from our clenched fists. Were they to ease the pain of leaving? We had strict instructions not to touch them until we were on the road. Johnny, a friend of ours, a mongol child, stood waving from his front door adorned even on this bright sunny day in his duffel coat, scarf and green balaclava. We recognised him by his big brown boots and his slightly revealed mischievous smile which could change to a wicked temper in a split second.

Our parents and granny came out and slowly our car moved off, Johnny's bulging figure soon easing into the clouds and then... nothing. Nothing but the unknown.

We were on our way, this big adventure, so far unmapped for us children; ours to face head on. Not long into the journey my brother and I started to fight. To be in such close proximity and not exchange a few blows seemed to fly in the face of tradition. We got a good slap for our antics.

I stood up all the way else I would see nothing. I looked behind us and watched the big grey rickety removal van attempt to keep up with us, great balloons of dirty smoke spitting out from its ancient body. It was only that morning that I had reluctantly packed away my toys into a tea chest. I didn't trust these men. I had to keep my eyes on them. There they were right behind us, trailing us as if attached by an invisible rope. I kept looking back every few minutes becoming more and more anxious at the thought of my favourite toys bouncing about alone in the back of this big monster driven by a man with milk-bottle glasses and a nervous tic. My anxiety turned to almost blind panic when I suddenly noticed the van had disappeared. That's it, I thought, my soul mates gone forever. My future life would have a destiny scribbled out for it without the warming comfort of my one eared teddy bear; my three wheeler with the metal bucket seat and only two wheels; the broken bicycle pump which made squealing noises if you used it with your lips attached. And my totally new and undamaged plastic football. All gone. My little mind thought it a miracle when we arrived in Forkhill to find the van sitting outside our new home.

Our journey had taken us through the then unfamiliar territory. Through Cloghue and its massive church peering down from on high; seeing Killeavey's football pitch off to the right, the big white goal posts stretching for the skies; and along the winding hawthorn clamped roads to Meigh, situated on the valley floor between Slieve Gullion and the Fathom Mountains.

Dromintee was next along the village route and the late nineteenth century chapel winked with an elegance through the bulging trees as we sped along towards our destiny: the village of Forkhill. On past 'Cement Murphy's' house, so called because of the break in the tarmac just outside their house revealing the unimpressive patch of cement. In the not too distant future we would visit both Dromintee and Mullaghbawn chapels on alternate Sundays as we tried to ensure, as good god fearing Catholics, we were seated comfortably in whichever chapel housed the priest who would fire his way through the sacraments with the speed of light.

But for now. For now we watched excitedly as we soared down the steep hill, bringing into view the village itself resting contentedly among the green and heathered mystic of Slieves Gullion and Brack; legends and myths cascading from their very peaks.

Mullaghbawn sat with a degree of arrogance over to the right a few miles, with its attractive setting in the broad valley between Slieve Gullion and the ring dyke hills. A now unused Church of Ireland place of worship rested between Forkhill and Mullaghbawn.

To my recollection there were only a few Protestants in the area at the time.

Then Crossmaglen. The now infamous Crossmaglen where Doctor Crommie kept his pill jars full of sweets for us ailing children and where once an African girl carried a wash basket on her head as we watched in amazement. For the life of me I cannot recall why she was in Crossmaglen. Further on and into the south of Ireland to be greeted by Dundalk. These places were to be my life and herald my fondest memories. Stretching like teasing mysteries were the many unofficial roads linking our divided country which were used with some success by the smugglers to outsmart the RUC. They were to cause my father much anguish and even more fun.

Today the beauty of this area refuses point blank to bow to the hooded corpses and dismembered bodies which have littered its laneways. In recent years it has held so many screams of tortured bodies. And indeed souls. Then, then just the easing sighs of undiluted pleasure.

I was so glad when we finally arrived in the village. The smell of the leather seats cooking under the midday sun coupled with the vision of crushed crisps resting on my lap had a good gossip behind my back with the pot-holed roads to make me feel more than a little nauseous. We had stopped three times on the way for me to make my mark on the countryside.

Chapter Two

Village life: that strange but unique and comforting environment, its territory grabbing you and transcending all other forms. To greet it is like a lost soul finding water after days of thirst. Villagers are by nature a calm and in the main friendly species, unaffected, it seems, by the strife or material seeking hands of other worlds. They will welcome you with a smile as wide as an ocean, while at the same time sizing you up. Villagers have a warmth and a subtle nosiness that welcomes the visitor and embraces the stayer with a strong grip.

The police barracks sat high at an angle off the road linking the main street with the Back Road, the village school but a shout away. Residing in the barracks were the other sergeant and his wife and family, while the constables, about seven in all and mainly young and unmarried, lived in less than five star conditions next door. A hefty multi-bolted door adjoined the sergeant's bedroom to the barracks. All the windows were barred and had been painted a sickly green a good few years back. The front door of the barracks also fell victim to the painter's green period.

Sandbags sheltered the entrance, a permanent fixture in case of the traditional periodic burst of IRA activity. Forkhill was not however an area normally associated with IRA campaigns. Camlough and Crossmaglen had had their share of Republican assaults on the 'Establishment'. Camlough, where the silvery lough grins at the gorsey landscape and which today has among its accepted residents many different and quite rare birds: the mute swan, great

9

crested grebes, moorhens and warblers. And Crossmaglen, with its vibrant market place and public houses offering their wares to coy market day farmers.

But yet Forkhill had seen the death of a policeman. Constable Henry Ross was cycling along a road near the village when a land mine exploded in a ditch in 1958. In November 1961, a few months into our first year in the village, I was to see my father come home one evening close to tears. A traditional period of IRA activity was about to be embedded in my young mind.

So there we were: my mother, father, granny and my brother and myself. My brother and I had rushed into the house to lay claim to our room. Waste of time, Granny got it. The house was cold and empty, our voices echoing in its soul, our breaths smoking even on this warm day. I went out into the back garden while the removal men got on with their work. The garden was overgrown, the path up the middle sprouting thick weeds. On spying our next door neighbours venture from their house I quickly dashed back into ours; this was a bit too early for formal introductions. Everyone seemed really happy in our new home and soon the cold of the house fell victim to the emerging fire and our voices. My mother kept on about the beautiful scenery, my father had gone round to the barracks for a crack. A book kept my granny occupied.

As a six year old I thought, okay, everything's fine. But where's the action?

"Tomorrow, you two are going up to have a look at your new school." My mother's words were not exactly what I had in mind.

It was the school holidays so although the school was obviously shut Mr Keating, the headmaster, soon to be called 'The Master' and quoted on everything from sums to frogspawn by my brother, had arranged to meet us. A typical village school presented itself, dreary from the outside with its flaky blistered white-washed walls. Inside the classrooms boasted various colourful drawings littering the walls, some better than others depending on the age of the room's usual inhabitants. My mother and Mr Keating chatted as we sat near the dormant pot bellied stove which would soon cause us intestinal nightmares as the teachers would use it to thaw out the bottled milk in the winter months. If unsuccessful they would add boiling water to the bottle resulting in tepid milk.

I can still smell its clutching odour.

So there it was, our prison for the next few years. The full details of this adventure had obviously not been explained to me in any great detail. I recalled my first day at school in Belfast queuing up in the yard, boys on one side, girls on the other. No mingling. Some of us giggling, some with tear stains etched on frightened little faces, others about to wet themselves.

I took no chances, I did the lot. My father took me to the toilet. It was such a relief. But I, at my tender age, could not be blamed for the mistake. My father should however have known better.

He took me into the girls' toilet. I should have accepted the warning and realised that school and I were a mis-match.

School always seemed unable to present a face of enjoyment. It was as if learning and fun couldn't be bed partners. It is often said that school days are the best of your life. Certainly the time spent having fun with your mates and the long summer holidays were to be recommended but the actual exercise of taking in knowledge and imparting it at various times both orally and on paper was much overrated.

The school in Forkhill boasted four teachers: Master Keating; Miss Larkin; Miss Gaughan who took the infants and Master Campbell who we later discovered was a distant relative. His expertise was woodwork. There wasn't a great deal separating their ages. The playground at the back of the school was a decidedly rough patch of ground that had long since given up on growing anything productive, like grass. The odd clump of watery green feathers halted the announcement of complete baldness and the rocks which jutted out at regular intervals did little to portray this as the ideal children's play area.

The toilets took their pride of place at the steps to the play area. Like many others I would rather hang on in there than use these facilities. They were disgusting and were seemingly never introduced to a cleaner and while the heavens opened on a regular basis and sluiced them now and again the overriding factor was the smell. Crows used to hang around them, obviously suffering from nasal blockages. We used to have to queue there every morning and afternoon. One morning I really needed to go badly, my bowels were being asked to work overtime. By lunchtime I was almost crippled but as I went home for lunch I needed just to hang on in there a little while more before I could take full advantage of our own spotlessly clean bathroom.

I made my way home, a less than five minute walk. Each movement however was like a punch in the bowels. I was about four hundred yards from home when the situation worsened to such a degree that remedial action was required. I stopped. Decision time. Nobody was about except for a few of Haughey's cows gazing at nothing in particular. They would have no room to complain, the mess they left.

Should I continue at this slow pace for the impending bowel explosion was causing me to walk as if on eggs, every step a carefully thought out movement? Or should I take the ultimate risk and run the remaining few yards home thus making my agony reach its conclusion sooner? If ever I had to write an essay on My Favourite Day this one would slip through the net.

I straightened up, took a deep breath and made my decision.

Boy did I get it wrong.

I was about two yards into a sprint when it happened. It's at times like this you pray for constipation; the good lord must have been deaf. I got the reverse. Now I was carrying extra baggage. I was forced to regroup my options and think again. Slowly. If I ran I could well produce an unwelcome trail alerting all and sundry to my predicament. No, I didn't want that. I'd die of shame. Instead I took on the bearing of an amateur John Wayne as I edged forward at less than a mile an hour, my final destination still in my tortured vision. On reflection I should perhaps have introduced a degree of realism to the scene.

Pretending I was on a horse and slapping my backside was for obvious reasons not to be recommended but firing off a couple of imaginary six shooters wouldn't have gone amiss.

Chapter Three

My father was now spending more and more time in the barracks and we got to see him only at lunch times when we came back from school. Unbeknown to him, on his first day in the village, the lads in the barracks arranged a bit of a surprise for him. 'Get to know the locals', sort of thing. One of the area's notorious smugglers sat outside the barracks with a lorry load of undoubtedly smuggled pigs.

"Grand day, sergeant," he greeted my father, then introduced himself.

"It is, indeed. It's nice to meet you. And if there is anything I can do for you..." my father had to raise his voice now as the pigs made it clear they were anxious to be off... "don't hesitate to get in touch." The smuggler waved goodbye and watched my father doff his cap and shake his head as the squealing began to echo throughout the village. My father had a lot to learn. Practice was something he wouldn't be short of. Many's the night we would be tucked up in bed while he struggled for supremacy with the smuggler.

Meanwhile my grandmother was getting her bearings and her great love, walking, was now taking her farther afield and invariably to her other love – the chapel. Often she would set off early in the morning, her walking stick to the fore, heading purposely in the direction of Dromintee just to say a few prayers or maybe the rosary. Like many of her generation she was frail, with a gentle nature coupled with a dry, almost wicked sense of humour.

Maybe the legacy of a really hard life where pride hid a lot of problems. She was a very private person who didn't easily mix although she did strike up a friendship with two elderly ladies, both Protestants, and they would share tea and digestive biscuits on a regular basis while they chatted about everything under the sun except religion. Not to offend, you see. Maybe that's been our problem in Ireland. We don't talk enough.

My grandmother's love of walking was to be her downfall, quite literally. My games of marlies with her after school would soon be curtailed. I would also miss her wicked habit of opening the front door without her false teeth and grinning maniacally. However, in the coming years her gummy expression would give fright to the soldiers residing next door. Had she been doing her bit for Ireland?

We soon located places of interest and for me that was exclusively the sweetshops. The closest was Lizzie Sleith's situated at the top of a trailing road leading to O'Neill's public house. Just before was 'Hop' Campbell's little white washed abode. On a Sunday people would travel for miles to hear Hop tell their fortunes, the gentle rushing of the river running alongside her house adding a degree of mystery to her prophecies. She was called Hop on account of the fact that she had a wooden leg and did in fact hop. No malice was attached to this name.

The proximity of Lizzie's shop was to be honest all it had going for it, for often the produce had a sell by date written in stone. A great advantage to us kids was the fact that if you asked for, say, a quarter of brandy balls you would be less than fortunate if you came away with less than a pound as they were stuck rigid with age. Lizzie being a person with a short fuse was never in a mood to prise them apart. The shop itself was joined to her living quarters and a rather hoarse tinkling bell alerted her to your presence. Lizzie suffered from a glandular problem and was grossly overweight. This obviously slowed her movements somewhat and it wasn't unusual for darkness to take over from daylight as she made her way out to stand behind the mahogany counter. To be met with a request for two flapjacks – total value, one halfpenny – did not endear you to her.

"Get out of my shop," she would roar. All this before 'customer service' blunted the natural anger of many shopkeepers. "Do you think I have nothing better to do?" We had no idea how her personal life went so were unable to offer a response.

I, as the Sergeant's son, never got such treatment. It appeared I was somehow different. I didn't want it to be that way and was pleased, believe it or not, the first time I was caned in school, the tingling of my little hand no match for the pride I suddenly felt I was accepted.

Further on down the craggy stone wall hugged road you encountered Thomas McCreesh's shop, a large seldom used store which at one time, legend had it, served chips, a complete novelty then. Hardly ever did we venture into that shop except when once Thomas seemed to take his shopkeeping role seriously and got in a new magic item. Pear ice lollies. They took us into another world, a world up till then an orange colour and taste only. Obviously if he set his mind to it Thomas was a bit of an innovator. He was also the local taxi driver and in between smoked near enough one hundred cigarettes a day. Sadly, Thomas is now gone.

The trail then took you to the pick of the bunch: Murphy's. It was our favourite and had a sheltered doorway where in later years we would sit huddled together munching crisps and swigging from brown lemonade bottles as outside in full view of us the snowy threads of winter cascaded. We shivered but felt strangely warm. Inside.

Murphy's had the best sliders in the village. Two crisp wafers crammed with creamy, blindingly white, ice cream. And all for three pence. For sixpence you would need your two hands free. Katherine Dooley owned another seldom used shop a few yards down the road past the pebble-dashed Courthouse where such crimes as fighting over land, stealing sheep and the procurement of poteen were dealt with. The shop was dark and poorly lit but did have some terrific yellow lucky lumps, a penny or two always seemed to be in them.

At the far end of the village was McCreesh's, the main store and visits there for confectionery fixes alone were few and far between. This is where we did the messages for our parents or anyone else who called on our services. As a child you would often be stopped by an adult. They always seemed to be peering through the curtains. On the lookout for us 'mini-adults'. You would be doing your best to evade the Red Indians chasing you or trying to bounce a ball of a wall and control it like George Best when they would get you. We were generally more than willing to go for messages because invariably you would be rewarded with a penny or two. Then you would have the luxury of this financial comfort ensuring a reasonable look round the shop. No rush. Deciding between a couple of gob stoppers or two or three lucky lumps, their yellow sparkles smiling from the jar. Maybe your pal would have a couple of pence and the combined purse would allow the purchase of a Cowan toffee bar, creamy to the taste.

Despite being better off financially than the rest of the village neither my brother nor I were spoilt with material things. We got the odd copper, or three pence now and again. Occasionally, sixpence. Material things didn't interest us despite our so called social standing. I recall once standing outside the dreaded toilets, trouble enough as you can imagine, when this boy was playing with a small toy helicopter. It was exactly the same colour as one I had.

"I've got one of those," I exclaimed.

"You have everything."

I hadn't but I suppose to many it seemed we had. No matter how close we got to the people, and I would like to think that to most we did, we were always going to be 'The Sergeant's sons' to some of our classmates. In Nationalist areas there has always been a distrust of the RUC, created and perhaps sustained, to a degree, by the force being traditionally drawn from the Protestant communities. A lack of communication on a daily basis didn't help. For instance the constables in Forkhill were from different parts of the North: Belfast, Fermanagh, Derry etc, and when they were off duty they returned home to their families. Contact, apart from the odd hello, was rarely explored. The sergeant and his predecessors would invariably have children of school age but they went to school in Newry. Whether they were ever invited to attend our school in Forkhill I don't know, likewise I am unaware of what their response might have been. So contact through children was never actually made. The fact that we were Catholics allowed us immediate contact through the horrors of school life.

I would like to think however that, wherever we were, both my father and mother would have made the effort to fit in. I seem to recall it was made easy in Forkhill. My father was a lover of a bit of crack and this made him available to everyone and anyone as he would spend many an hour just sauntering around the village, cap to the back of his head, his uniform carefully brushed, making contact with the locals both young and old. My mother did her shopping in McCreesh's whereas the other sergeant's wife would shop in Newry, the nearest big town, when bringing the kids back from school. There was no direct animosity towards the police but I think my father's style of policing set up a trust destroyed only by his departure from Forkhill and the advent of the troubles.

Coming from a large Protestant family in Coleraine I don't think he found anything easy in life and adopted a rather simple way of dealing with things. Talk. Leaving school at an early age like so many, he become disillusioned with his first job, as a brickie, and successfully applied to join the RUC, much to the delight of his aunt Jinny who brought the family up single-handed after the early death of my grandparents. As a raw recruit he was posted to Ballynahinch, his first station in a series of eight.

A posting to the seaside town of Warrenpoint brought him into regular contact with a small corner shop wherein my mother worked. My father converted to Catholicism and my parents soon married and honeymooned in the tranquillity of Donegal. Both of them had the naivety of ignorance really I suppose, as neither of them really understood how religion in Ireland could have any bearing on how people treated you. They were soon to find out.

On return from Donegal my father turned up for duty at Warrenpoint to be told that he was being transferred to Carrickfergus. Immediately. There were no married quarters available so it was obvious (particularly to the authorities) that my mother could not join him. He spent months pushing for a move and eventually secured Crossmaglen, another 'bog station'. A favourite resting place for the few Catholic policemen in the Force or for anyone who had blotted their copybook in anyway. My father had been a Protestant, converted, and then married a Catholic. I think they threw his copybook away. Little did they know that the many policemen who passed through the 'shame of the bog stations' will tell you of the great times they had there.

My parents set up home in Urker House, a farmhouse owned by the famous horse people, the Kiernans. My grandmother joined them having sold her small home in Warrenpoint, the purchase of which was possible through the hard work she put into the family farm at Glasker. My maternal grandfather was less than useless according to popular opinion. Even when his face was out of a pint pot.

Their home had neither light nor water, candles flickered as the day faded and water had to be brought from two fields away. A school teacher and his wife, Pop and Gee, as we affectionately named Mr and Mrs Magee, lived next to us and became life long friends. A friendship slightly sullied only in later years when Gee regularly cut both my brother's and my hair. This was at a time when long hair was beginning to become fashionable.

"Is that enough off?" she would ask of my mother as our almost bald scalps shone in the sunlight peeking through the curtains.

"Bit more, the teachers at Violet Hill insist on short hair."

Do they indeed? I thought. Maybe if I insisted on piddling on this carpet you might not be so willing to keep cutting. Maybe if I ran away from home and slept in a ditch until my hair grew you'd worry about me and never cut my hair again.

Thoughts never changed the world so I went back to school each time, scaldy.

Sadly Pop is now dead but Gee endured the frowns and scowls and quivering lips to stay friends. Each and every Christmas before we got married my brother and I would receive a pound from her. I married late.

Crossmaglen saw my parents out in the fields growing their own vegetables, and in the bright cool spring evenings they would venture out and pick lettuce and scallions while my granny cooked wheaten and treacle bread on the griddle. It was a time I never tired of hearing.

Crossmaglen was another South Armagh stronghold and once again many friends were made there. The fact my father was a convert followed him everywhere and on the day he was transferred to Belfast he had to drag his heavy trunk from the station to the waiting landrover as three of his colleagues stood by, sneers scarring their sad lives. Such were the feelings of some to the converted. A certain Catholic shopkeeper in Warrenpoint refused to place change into my mother's hand for fear of touching her contaminated skin such was the reaction to her role in this absolute shamefaced deed.

They seemed however to enjoy life. In the slow lane, as my father would often say. My brother and I arrived a couple of years later at Newry hospital during their spell in Crossmaglen. Crossmaglen plays little part in my memory but it is still a place where my mother is made welcome. Not bad for an RUC man's wife in an area daubed as ungovernable by the media.

My father's police career was to be as varied as it was interesting and as I grew up he took great pleasure in telling me about it. A pleasure I felt in listening. He once told be about the time he was not long out of Enniskillen (RUC training school) when he was checking for tillage (which was keeping an eye on farmers to ensure that the level of weeds on their land was kept down). He was called into the farmer's house at about nine in the morning for a bite of breakfast. The bite of breakfast in fact manifested itself in the dark form of stout poured to the top of a glass and pushed into my father's willing but slightly dubious hand. He was after all a policeman first and a potential drunk second.

He consumed second and third helpings and then, realising the task in hand, struggled to his feet with the help of the farmer and his wife. Reaching the field in question he gazed across its weed ravaged vastness and noticed a goat munching happily in the corner. With a stupid grin on his face and a slur both in his voice and movements he dandered over to the goat who was a friendly sort. And hungry.

As my father dozed in the morning sunlight, the consumption of stout encouraging his snoring, the goat dined on his notebook containing details of the whole week's tillage count.

Another time during the last war while the Germans bombed Belfast he and his colleagues frantically searched debris pulling out survivors and the dead. My father found one man, his legs sticking out from under a pile of bricks. Unsure as to whether he was alive or not he pulled at the body and it slowly came through. Headless.

An IRA man with a bomb presented a different kind of challenge. My father talked him out of doing anything with it and received a medal for his actions to which he paid little heed. I think it's buried somewhere in a drawer at home.

Now here in Forkhill he was about to chase smugglers and dodge feuding farmers, and on occasion attend our school to instruct us on road safety. My brother and I would arrange these visits to coincide with a class we didn't like. We were becoming useful to the locals. The class we wanted to miss would invariably be woodwork taken by Master Campbell's successor who was a complete and utter failure as a teacher and as a human being. He got his kicks from humiliating us kids. He was young, and that originally appealed to us. Apparently he played gaelic for Armagh now and again but drink took him over. Still, why take it out on a few of us?

I recall once at Christmas time when we were all obviously excited, not least because of the long break from school, when this particular teacher decided that the fun we, or rather he, would have that day before we broke up would be for all of us to sing a song in front of the whole class. Most of us were petrified at the thought, many of us considering trying to cram into needlework classes with the girls.

I couldn't sing to save my life, I didn't know any songs yet on hearing Gene Smith singing/humming, I don't think he had made his mind up, the tune to an advert for Rolos, a chocolate caramel sweet, I thought that would do for me. I persuaded Gene to hand over to me the singing rights for the next day.

"I know some of you are worried about singing so don't worry I won't ask you to," he said to us all but smiled at me in particular as he entered the classroom next day. An audible sigh of relief surged from many a tense body for there were a number of us who had season tickets to shyness. He's not really that bad, I thought, and a few of us, the ones with voices like pregnant whales in a tight supermarket queue, winked at each other. Christmas was something to really look forward to now. We all listened to a good few songs emitting from yet to break voices, the odd giggle or two harmonising with at times rather dulcet tones. I was staring out the window, it was the last class of the day. Freedom was circulating all round the school. I could smell it. A couple of minutes to go. Some of us were beginning to pack away our things. The singing stopped, the last red faced lad sat down and breathed a sigh of relief. There were indeed a few of us with whom he hadn't bothered.

"Before you all go," he began getting up from his seat, "I would like to wish you a very happy Christmas. One last thing before you go... I think we should hear Master White's offering." My heart sank. I looked round me, heads dropped. The teacher smiled.

I cannot recall the words of the advert even though I think it was about a two liner but you can imagine the sophistication of it, all those years ago. I can however recall the burning of my face, the deathly quiet as my unleashed voice peppered the classroom and upset the plants no doubt. And all the time he sat staring at me, a sneering grin on his face. When I had finished, and Rolo's sales were about to plummet, he just waved us all out of the room.

Another time, for reasons which escape me, a number of us who played in the Under 12s gaelic team went on strike. I think it had something to do with the training he had us doing. In his class he tried to break us down, and over a period of a few weeks we did weaken, a few of the lads breaking down in tears. I wasn't far behind them but managed to hold on until I got home, and later in the day produced the waterworks.

It took a while for my parents to get out of me what was wrong. When they did they asked the teacher to come and see me. Everything was sorted out and he was very pleasant. Why couldn't he always be like this?

Next day in class as we neared the end of the lesson he rose. "I would just like to say that I am pleased the problems over the football team are now sorted out." He looked straight at me, not a smile creasing his face. "It's a pity though that Master White had to do his crying in front of his mammy."

With that he walked out of the room. I was very young to hate. But I hated that individual and still do to a degree.

Chapter Four

School, as you can imagine was not my favourite place. An unnecessary evil if ever there was one. As soon as you walk through the doors as a frightened four year old they ply you with visions of secondary school, university and if you're really clever: You could become a teacher.

Technically, therefore, you could spend the waking hours from the age of four until you were about sixty five in SCHOOL. And this was encouragement. Parole, it appeared, came about only with bad behaviour.

It is a long held belief of mine when we part these uninspiring shores for the last time and end up in Hell, God should re-open the case against us and take into account the years spent behind educational bars. My suspicions, as I have already mentioned, should have been aroused to the horrors in store following the less than auspicious start in the Holy Child School in Belfast. There, the first couple of days appeared to dilute my initial fears somewhat. Plasticine provided freedom of imagination and as a four year old I had imagination in abundance; unfortunately my creative skills knew no new moves and all my attempts at making animals, houses, my teacher, even, turned out in the shape of dog's mess.

And my teacher insisted in calling me Sean.

Now I've nothing against the name itself. It's just that it isn't mine. I have had this problem all my life especially in England. The English, god bless them for they are a simple race, consider you must be called Sean if you're Irish. One or two have even asked me am I sure my name isn't Sean? Apart from producing my birth certificate, I suggested they take my word for it!

The plasticine and the toys were great and edging towards friendship as the days passed was enticing. Then... "Children, please look at the blackboard. What do you see?" Questions. I hadn't been warned.

I saw loads of squiggly shapes which I later identified as letters frowning down at us. Pieces of paper were rested on our desks and big thick black-leaded pencils completed the less than attractive ensemble. One or two of us began to cry, the boy next to me wet himself and cried out loudly. Fair comment, I thought. We had to copy these shapes. A-B-C-D...

On my first day at school in Belfast my father brought me to school. In Forkhill it was just my brother and I traipsing up the straight hedged Back Road to our destiny. I wanted to hold Leo's hand but didn't. My shiny new school bag slung over my shoulder was cutting into me and my breathing was affected. I was like an old hunchbacked man making my way to school.

I was assigned to Miss Larkin's class, Leo to 'The Master's'. The only person I really knew, and fought with most of the time, was now out of reach as I sat beside another boy whose nose was running and whose handkerchief wasn't running as fast. The two-seater desks were etched with use over the years, stained with god knows what, and maimed with pock-marks inflicted with what must have been something resembling a pneumatic drill. Probably just a dedicated soul with a nibbed pen.

A couple of girls smiled at me from afar. Gummy mouths in no way hiding genuine friendliness. But this was no time for fraternizing with the enemy; my greatest fear at being sat beside a girl didn't materialise so I was in no mood for eye contact with girls. It could lead to all sorts of accusations. Firstly, I had to endeavour to win over the respect and admiration of my male colleagues. The room smelt strongly of stale milk spilt from a previous life and yet to be convinced of its demise. The pot bellied stove rumbled convincingly at the front of the room despite it being quite a warm September.

I wondered what Leo was doing? Was my mother in the house?

Was Granny on her way to Dromintee? And was my father in his official capacity discussing with his loyal constables a secretive plot to rescue his youngest from a hell not of his own making? Were they at this very moment loading the landrover with heavy artillery in case of resistance from Miss Larkin? And then I thought...

Could I trust a man who on my first day at school led me into the girls' toilets?

Despite an excess of school attendance the weeks rolled quite easily into months and things were beginning to settle down. In the beginning at school I used to rush out and run home as quickly as I could not feeling able to join in with the rest. But soon a child's natural taste for fun and adventure forced me to link up with my classmates on the short journey home. Free from the confines of walls and education. As a group we put on the usual after school pantomime designed probably to the onlooker as something for the sub-normal.

Basic shoving and punching began on immediate release from the chains of our two times tables and the prophetic rantings of our teachers: "If you don't listen carefully, you'll be nothing when you grow up." We would then run down the road whacking our backsides to the imaginary western film playing vividly in our limitless imagination. Shots being fired from smoking index fingers. Haughey's docile cud chewing cattle taking the brunt of it. Audie Murphy and John Wayne were constant visitors to the Back Road. If feeling slightly less energetic we would just chuck each other into the nettle infested hedgerow or try to strangle some unsuspecting soul bending down to tie his laces.

Sometimes we would stop for a while and see who could spit the furthest; to facilitate accurate detection of these oral emissions we would chew great lumps of grass prior to lift off. Other times we would just stand and stare over Haughey's rusty gate taking in the daisy marked fields. And the cows. God, in his last will and testament, must have bestowed exclusive rights to tranquillity to Haughey's cows for they used to lie there dozing or chewing. Amid the deep, deep yellow of the bobbing buttercups they mulled over life. We would eventually get home to totally unworried parents. What had they to worry about?

Chapter Five

We had an inherent respect for adults, particularly old people. Having said that, they in turn treated us like fellow human beings, albeit a bit shorter. Next door to us lived a quiet elderly couple, the Kirks. Mrs Kirk was blind and suffered from an ailment now medically termed as Alzheimer's disease. Then, then it was just a case of an old person 'doting'. She talked to herself and waved her hands frantically in the air as her mind took her back along the familiar route to the safety of childhood. In the summer months she would sit out the back with the sun caressing her fragile mind; we used to laugh, as kids do, at her mumblings and gesticulations. She eventually ended up in a Home and we got to know Mr Kirk better when she died. He was a strong proud man and had once served in the RIC. A well built man with a thick dark nicotine tainted moustache contrasting sharply with his snow white hair.

He smoked like a trooper and wasn't opposed to the odd bottle of stout which my mother collected for him from Quinn's Off-Licence in Newry where she did his shopping. It wasn't exactly the done thing for a woman to visit such establishments in those days. Didn't seem to bother my mother then. Certainly it doesn't bother her now.

Mr Kirk trusted both my brother and I; he didn't really know anyone else and we would do the odd bit of local shopping for him. His tall frame would fill his doorway as he called to us while we were out scoring goals for Manchester United in the European Cup Final. He was a very private person who used to regale us with tales of his RIC days. I was too young to really understand and enjoy. A pity. He gave me a half crown for my first Holy Communion, a small fortune. I liked the man and not just for that. He was what I now know to be a gentleman, then I knew him as a gentle man.

Religion played a big part in our lives. We were not the sort to 'lick the altar rails' but nonetheless being a Roman Catholic meant close affinity to god and the chapel. Or at very least, the appearance of such. Now I was as good a Catholic as the next, but I did find this trekking to chapel every Sunday a bit of a bore, especially when the mass was in Latin. Then I hadn't a clue what was going on although we did have translation missals in later years.

Even then I failed to grasp what was going on. Then, I was having enough trouble getting to grips with the English language without the added burden of following mass in a dead language. I had mastered the basics of what was not exactly my mother tongue but which now gave me the means to communicate to others what I wanted. 'Can I have..?' was a term I took to quite readily and practiced at every given opportunity but frequently without the desired effect. To my amazement I was soon coming out with expressions adults thought were cute. Why you're thought of as cute and amusing at that age and nosey and 'too grown up' years later was baffling?

My reading and writing was stepping up a pace and my father let me use the typewriter in his office. I loved being in there watching him work. It was cramped to say the least, with a small always cluttered desk facing the barred windows. Behind the desk rested an old iron wrought chair over which lay my father's black tunic, usually at an angle. His silver whistle hanging loosely. An antiquated jet black telephone sat on its large rest, tinkling now and again. Glaring from the corner was a three barred fire, a large glass of cold water standing by to offset the stuffiness. Next door, in a locked cupboard, sterling sub-machine guns and rifles slept in the quietness of peace.

Using one finger only my father would painstakingly complete reports, only occasionally were proceedings livened up with the courage of a two fingered assault.

He managed it though and would often let me apply the seal to envelopes, the waxy red substance clinging to my hands. I would sometimes sit on his lap adding a further obstacle to his work. I loved it. Now and again he would let me loose on the typewriter. At first I would just sit there, tongue sticking out, concentration in first gear, and type any letters which came into my head. I found the magic of appearing forms fascinating especially if I pumped one letter continuously. Before long this practice was enabling me to venture into the actual formation of words which I knew or copied from some book.

"Try your name," my father suggested.

Various attempts resulted in misplaced letters innocent of any real semblance of the language: 'Shen Hite'; 'Sane Hit' appeared at various intervals. I practiced and practiced, my tongue going further out while my index finger poked the letters in a new found determined fashion.

At last I was successful; I managed to get it on paper. Triumphantly I pulled the sheet from the typewriter not giving it a chance to muck things up. Rushing up to my father I pushed the paper into his hand searching anxiously into his eyes for signs of approval and pride to which I felt entitled.

A slow smile crept into his face as he looked at me, then the paper. The smile built up, I could tell he was proud of me, wasn't he? He passed the paper to a few others who were unable to suppress their laughter.

Admittedly Shane Shite was not my exact name but I did try.

As already mentioned we as a family used to chase the fastest priest, whether it be in Mullaghbawn or Dromintee. Fathers Connelly and McDonald were the swift ones. This carefully planned procedure was shattered when visiting missionary priest came to educate us on their work abroad. Ones from Peru who hadn't a clue about 'South Armaghisms' were a constant source of anguish.

Normally however we had to negotiate only our usual priests. Our precision planning, which just fell short of actually ringing up the priests in question for confirmation of their whereabouts, could be knocked sideways if we were presented with the awesome figure of one Father Jordon from Jonesborough. He had this habit of stressing before the offertory collection that his ears were tuned to the different sounds of buttons and coins hitting the plate. I suppose a few of the locals could rest easily knowing that they would not have to secure their trousers manually after having donated to the good priest.

Father Jordon was the original fire and brimstone merchant, a massive frame squeezed into the pulpit, spittle accompanying almost every syllable. Shouting and crashing his hands on the pulpit completed his act. 'God; Damnation; Burning in hell etc' were oft quoted. He scared me, and no doubt woke up a few of the congregation. Death was another word often spouted and we were left in no doubt that this life on earth was but a preparation for the after life; this indeed is the teachings of the Christian religions. But we were only kids. Death, we couldn't even spell it. It was soon however to slam into our lives.

I have no doubt that some adults attended mass through fear. It was a mortal sin not to attend mass as it was to take someone's life. I had problems with that even at a young age. You had to be really ill to miss mass. I remember one Saturday night I was suffering from terrible earache. I was in agony. My mother spent most of the night telling me a story about a rabbit (if only I could remember it) which kept me entranced for a good few hours with only the odd crying session when the pain ignored the story. The next day the pain subsided; sleep had provided the extra medicine topping up the injection of the rabbit story. I stayed in bed and missed mass. Late afternoon I felt well enough to come down for dinner. Sitting with my brother eating I heard my father come through the front door. His face ashen and his open palms shaking as he held them up in the air. My mother's hands went to her mouth. They talked in voices laced with fear as the television splintered their utterings. I really wasn't interested anyhow.

Later I was to learn that my father and his patrol had been ambushed by the IRA after setting up a check point outside the Church of Ireland church in Jonesborough, overlooking the Newry-Dundalk road and nudging the beautiful forest nearby. The lads had set up the sten gun facing out of the back of the landrover when suddenly bullets lashed into them from the church grounds. Big Willie Hunter, a gentle giant of a man, fell to the ground mortally wounded. One bullet hit him. Most of the other patrol members were hit. My father escaped as he quickly realised what had happened and threw himself to the ground, shouting to his colleagues. But most of them were stunned into immobility.

Big Willie lay dead as the throes of shock hit some of the other lads. My father often mentioned how glad he was that he stood in for Big Willie on guard duty the previous night to allow him to see his girlfriend.

So that was my first introduction to death. I recall this woman from Forkhill whose husband was buried in the church grounds complaining that the gunmen had trampled over his grave. Religion to different people seemed to take on a very strange face at times.

The chapel at Dromintee was built in 1870 on the prominent glacial tail of Slieve Gullion. Even as a not particularly interested child I could still feel the warmth and comfort exuding from these grand surroundings. The building had presence. Beautiful hand carved stations of the cross depicting Jesus' suffering looked on quietly, making way on each side of the church for the dark-wooded, foreboding confessional boxes. I sometimes accompanied my family as they went to confession, watching people huddled into the pews praying before it was their turn. Or maybe because it was their turn. Almost total silence cuffed the whole area, nothing could be heard from within the clasping doors except for the gossiping whispers as prayers were mouthed and the synchronised twiddling of rosary beads.

Even then I could feel a sense of its importance, even though I couldn't fully comprehend what was going on or the exact function of these little boxes. I was of course told but couldn't master the techniques and the consequences of these visits. The priest seemingly had two people in with him at the same time. Whatever he said to them when they came out they would be down praying and blessing themselves like it was going out of fashion. Some for long periods, others far shorter. If anyone was in with the priest for a long time they were stared at when they came out. What was he/she up to? Murder, no doubt. Or maybe bunking mass?

It was a world to which I was soon to be introduced.

Mullaghbawn chapel was a more modern establishment with a

much less weed cluttered graveyard. It was situated at the bottom of a very steep hill and in the slippery days of winter it provided the faithful with a stern test of their beliefs as they tried to get up it to go home. Father McGuinness, the parish priest and slow with it, would glide down the hill in his car accompanied in the back seat by his housekeeper. No contact with the opposite sex for priests, which obviously included keeping a safe distance in broad daylight and in front of hundreds from his housekeeper. She always looked half strangled in her chin securing scarf.

Chapter Six

At mass, as in the car, I stood up to follow the proceedings, as indeed did most my age. Scattered about the place of worship were little swaying souls bobbing like restless buoys in an otherwise calm sea. Boredom caught you quickly, I think it was the silence that got to us. If we had been able to shout, scream and fight with big sticks we would have been okay but apparently it wasn't appropriate to engage in such activities in the Lord's house.

There were however a variety of things you could do but each had to be measured in terms of parental reaction. Standing on the wooden kneeling pad, holding on tightly to the front pew knocking some woman's scarf a touch in front was just about acceptable as long as you didn't overdo it. Ideally our parents would have preferred it if we had been able to stand on the ground, out of view.

Listening to the orchestral rumblings of those around us who had fasted since the early hours in order to receive Holy Communion was a favourite pastime. Stifling the giggles was a less enjoyable task. I can still get the giggles in the quietness of church. Speech was not allowed in chapel, not even whispering.

'Be quiet' was often mouthed at you if you decided to climb an imaginary flight of stairs by standing up and down on the kneeling pad. You got to about the third stair when you got the tug. All innocent you turned round to find out what was troubling the parent. In return you got a stern look and would be mouthed again. The parents had to be careful though for at the end of the day we really had the upper hand. Invariably you would be wearing fairly decent clothing to attend mass, even something brand new. Following the tug and the obligatory resistance from you, in accordance with the unwritten agreement among your fellow half pint strugglers, the parent had to be careful to ensure their control without stretching garments enough to fit a herd of cows. You, in turn, had to gauge how far you could stretch their patience or the garment concerned.

If you really felt confident you could test the waters further and receive the 'tug and push' routine.

This involved the aforementioned followed swiftly by a quick jerk of your head forcing your immediate concentration to centre on the dusty chapel floor, allowing the parent to issue instructions. You had to give them credit, they could whisper succinctly through clenched teeth. A breed of ventriloquists, parents.

"If you do that again I will smack the legs off you. Now behave, you're in chapel." This action did not technically break the no speaking rule for we would both be out of sight of the priest, our faces pressed hard together. Warnings and resistance meeting head on.

To be honest you could be pretty sure you wouldn't have your legs smacked off you if only for the fact that the reverborating consequences of such an action would immediately alert the entire congregation to the area of trouble. And we small people wouldn't be blamed. Oh, no.

"Can't control their kids in mass" would be the tutting accusation.

Sitting down at this stage was to be recommended, absolute stillness for a while didn't go amiss either. You could just have a bit of a look around at the various headgear adorning the womenfolk. Some wore hats but generally the requirement for them to have their heads covered was answered with the appliance of the scarf. A wide perusal was worthwhile particularly in winter months when the wearer would forget to loosen the scarf on entering the chapel and nearly choke on the way up to communion. A recent perm also had the scarf stretching high above the head like the corner point of a floral tent.

We children had a great gift for spotting the ridiculous, especially when such a wide range of people were available as they were at mass. That is if we had time in between sticking our tongues out to see who had the blackest following a session on Black Jacks, a liquorice sweet. Or, if things were racing towards boredom, we would try and see who could get their tongue the furthest up a nostril and then if we weren't spotted by the parents we would go for a double nostril. No favours or concessions were allowed for those with heavy colds.

The offertory bells signalled the time to take hold of the penny or threepenny bit given to you a few minutes earlier by the parent. You held it tightly in your little hand awaiting the arrival of the plate or raffia style basket. Of course the exertion of holding on tightly to the currency leaving one hand only to engage in the aforementioned activities was fraught with problems. Something had to give and invariably it was the coin.

The silence of the chapel played host to the sudden clinking sounds of wayward coins bouncing about the floor, hot off the hand. You got the look. The 'wait till I get you home' kind.

Panic drilled through us. The first priority was to establish the immediate location of the missing coin. A quick duke down on the floor was a must, resulting in immediate coughing and spluttering on coming into contact with the dust-disturbed stone floor. Your eyes started to water, thus lessening clear vision. Pure instinct took over, that and a blinding fear of the consequences should your mission be unsuccessful.

Finding yourself now in among the feet. Now as we all know these appendages come in all shapes and sizes but in a lifetime we would be unlucky if we had to actually look at more than a few at close range. Alas, this was not the case on a Sunday, when looking for coins. If you were lucky you would only come across the smelly ones or the odd joker who kicked you while you were down. Scrambling under seats, your eyes, your seeking hands, as they ghosted along in search of the elusive penny as the rattle of the offertory plate was reaching a crescendo. Sweat tripped from our cherubic features. Little can be said at this stage apart from...

Bunions.

Bunions of all shapes and sizes, some honed to a preferred formation, others neglected, taking on the appearance of craggy mountains. Our naked hands touched them as owners removed footwear to allow some stale air to circulate round the pulsating lumps. The feet were sweaty from the walk to mass. Contact!

The feeling was warm, round and hard, not unlike the missing coin. But it was throbbing. Not unlike a foot with bunions. I froze at the realisation and crawled back to my seat. Defeated. Red faced from both embarrassment and exertion but with the feelings of bunions still clinging to my hands.

At last the words 'Dominus vobiscum et cum spiritu tuo'. Even I understood this bit of Latin, roughly translated it meant time to go home. Home to lightly boiled eggs, the yolks almost blinding you as they shone in their white sky and plain bread with that lovely burnt crust, toasting at the beaming doric stove. Butter would then slide teasingly from their darkened base on to your eager hands. It was my job to do the toast, a task I really enjoyed in the cold winter months as I placed the fresh bread on a long thin fork and held it against the blazing fire. Soon my red face fought with the glowing embers for vividness, but I loved doing this. I loved the warmth, both from the fire and the fact that we were all together in the same house, huddling against the cold. Voices splintering the warm silence. I couldn't identify it then but this was what family life meant; the very simple things giving the most pleasure.

Like sticking the fork in my brother and looking all innocent as the accusations were fired at me.

If my father was with us all was well, and he usually tried to be there if only to crack open our eggs before we devoured the creamy eggy flavour that all eggs had then.

A big drawback to Sundays, however, was the fact that you had to wear good clothes. All day. This cut back drastically on the type of activities you could expect to lay before the day. Play was invented for children of my age; my imagination, my playground. Cut knees, fractured arms, they were all to come but in the meantime...

Chapter Seven

In no time at all it seemed, I was moving up and out of Miss Larkin's class and into Master Keating's. Miss Larkin was a thin ageing woman whose teaching methods were, to me at any rate, from another age. The fear factor coming into being. She would whack you across the knuckles with the edge of a ruler and she did this regularly to one lad simply because he was left handed, something considered not quite proper. A bit like murder and not going to mass on a Sunday, I suppose. This lad also had a stutter which as you can only imagine was not helped by this constant physical abuse, which quite rightly would not be tolerated today. Miss Gaughan used to inflict punishment on her pupils, ages ranging from four to about seven or eight, with the assistance of those big black obese cigar like pencils. There is no doubt in my mind that I didn't get slapped often because of who my father was. I mean I was no tear away but then neither were any of my classmates. The sins against the teacher which commonly attracted the abuse were: talking in class, failure to supply a correct answer to a question and, in Miss Larkin's case, if you brought in a big blackthorn stick for her to use. We had yet to learn the intricacies of algebra but we soon cottoned on to the equation – bringing in stick equals slap on the hand.

None of us had any real sympathy for the provider of the thorny means of educating us and now when I think back I reckon Miss Larkin had little respect for the individual concerned, maybe that's why she caned him or her first. Him, rather, for I cannot recall the girls getting slapped.

This sort of abuse I have to admit was not rife, not like in later years at St Coleman's secondary school where the teachers, mainly priests, appeared to vent their real or imagined frustrations on you. It was there however and unfortunately the same people fell victim time and time again.

There were a couple of lads from over Mullaghbawn way, farmer's sons who, together with their sister, attended our school. They all had a lovely dark complexion, obtained out in the fields I suppose. The two lads were constantly in trouble for not doing their homework. Time spent doing homework was valuable time lost in the upkeep of the farm. They often pleaded that they meant to do the work in the morning before school but forgot. More likely was that they were too busy bringing the cows in for milking to have time for school work. The sister obviously had her chores to do but perhaps at a more regulated time; the washing, doing the dishes etc. I suppose the parents thought that the natural progression of things would bring the lads into the farm and the sister would probably marry and the need for a formal education was not really necessary. An understandable feeling in such a community but nonetheless an unfortunate one which disallowed children from reaching their full potential. An education for the girl would do her no harm even if tradition did not allow her to use it.

Many's the time the two lads would not make an appearance for days and this would lead to the arrival of the 'Mitching Officer'.

"The School Attendance Officer is coming tomorrow." Words that would put the fear of god up them, that is if they were there. We all looked at the two lads for we knew what their reaction would be.

Wailing and gnashing of the teeth had nothing on these two. Their faces would screw up into tortured visors with sounds emitting like some legendary monster with toothache.

"Ah, Jaysus, no, sir. What are we going to do?" they would plead. Little sobbing figures would fold their arms on the dirty wooden ink stained desk and sob loudly, all hope gone, their shoulders moving like a disturbed ocean wave. There was no consoling them and they faced this ordeal alone, for I do not recall any notes from the parents explaining their absence.

We found it funny then, I found it funny for many a long year since but now that I recall it and write about them I can feel only sympathy for them. Through no fault of their own they had to mitch school.

Holy Communion was looming on the horizon and ready to pounce on most of us. "You had better know your Catechism," was a threat oft chucked in our direction. Soon we were to be bombarded with "Who made the world?" to which we would reply as one, parrot fashion,

"God."

"Who is god?"

"The Creator, and King, and Lord, and the Owner of Heaven and Earth, and all things."

"How many gods are there?"

"There is but one god who will reward the good and punish the evil."

Soon we were rolling these phrases and many more off our innocent tongues, not having a clue what the hell we were talking about but again feeling the fear if we were unable to grasp everything being crammed into our clear minds; an oasis for knowledge. It just seemed to be something we had to do and god help us if we didn't. It was to be the first really major experience in our short lives. It should have meant more. It could have been more fun without sacrificing the obvious solemnity of the occasion.

Like all of my age fun was what life was all about. Fun was life, life was fun. At school I never really enjoyed break times for we were still in the confines of school and the teachers were still watching us. So often today I hear children saying they are bored as they lie on their beds in their stereo adorned bedrooms, watching TV, as headphones blare into young ears, forcing knee and various arm movements reminiscent of permanent cramp.

Bored! We never knew the meaning of the word. There again, we never knew the meaning of being frightened outside, or of having to be careful who we spoke to. We were very lucky.

None of us liked school but accepted it as a way of life until something better came along. Getting out of school we were off. I have already mentioned some of the activities we engaged in on release. But as we aged our games got more sophisticated. We would dander off down the road, our satchels swinging in time with our spirits. For some reason much of our vocal emissions were not words taught through school but ones we seemingly stole from the animal world.

'YO, YO, YIP, YAH, AAGGH, WHOA, EEH, RIDE EM COW-BOY, QUACK, QUACK.' and variations on these. Permutations resulting sometimes in the use of the word: BUGGER.

As we knew we shouldn't be using this word it was a useful addition to our finely honed repertoire. We used to whisper this one, best to be on the safe side.

If anyone had sweets they would automatically share. Day old half sucked boiled sweets required a little time to unravel from the dusty cupboard that was the pocket of someone's duffel coat; we were dedicated little souls and didn't know the meaning of surrender not while there was still some life in that sweet. Once unravelled we would surround its owner who was of course entitled to the first go and would hopefully remove the remaining fluff with a good suck. It was then passed along the line going from mouth to mouth supplemented in some cases by bits of chewing gum which we pulled from the tarmac spitting out the bits of grit. All in all a reasonable start to the day.

We loved all weathers: snow, rain and sunshine. They were there to be enjoyed. When the sun shone it sparkled from its home in the sky looking down at you blinking in its presence, like a caring hand from another world. There were always stones to be thrown having been baked gently in the afternoon sun. Usually we threw them at girls in a nearby field who were picking yoke topped daisies, as the gentle breeze ruffled their flowery dresses, ready to make daisy chains. Amid them stood fluttering dandelions showing off their full golden pedigree. We scoffed at the girls. If the truth be known our sneering reflected our inability to construct such delicate items.

No, not for us such childish, girlish activities. Our actions were of a more sophisticated nature.

We had snatched satchels to jump up and down on with the hope that an uneaten apple was still in residence.

Spring allowed long treks down Orney Loanen amid the

blackberry laced hedges, gorging yourself with the sweet berry. Watching the new born lambs tottering innocently near their mothers, oblivious to their inevitable fate. Shy big eyed calves looked at you suspiciously as you leaned over a fence calling 'cluck, cluck' to them. A sudden movement and they jerked away, long spindly legs moving out of unison. Or gazing spellbound at the multi-coloured butterflies fluttering like ribbons in the wind, settling now and then to allow a closer look as they lifted their delicately carved wings, seemingly preening themselves. Or showing off.

Unblemished skies towered overhead as village life yawned to spring's lifeline having trudged through winter's heavy darkened hand. Summer was in fact just a follow on from spring, only thing was that you had more time off school.

Autumn and winter provided that cosy feeling as you wandered the streets heavily wrapped up in duffel coats, gloves and maybe an additional visor: the dreaded knitted balaclava. Fighting the swirling autumn burnt leaves with an imaginary sword as you re-enacted the story of one of the knights of old kept you occupied for hours. Winter laid out slippery paths as you screeched arrogantly along on your hunkers before ending up on your backside, frantic laughter impeding your progress. Home made sleighs, unfit for sitting on never mind taking a bend, were put into action as our screams of joy melted into the snow clad days or gently mingled with the sun's rays. Whatever or whenever, it was fun. The games we played innumerable and so varied.

Chapter Eight

"Mammy, mammy, I'm home," you would utter a superfluous scream as you threw your satchel in the corner, banging doors in case your vocal announcement had been missed. Grabbing a glass of milk or one of granny's digestives I was ready for the off. Usually when I got home dad was on duty, out in the landrover somewhere or sailing gently around the countryside on his trusty bike. Whatever mode of transport in use you could be sure he made frequent stops for a crack. Granny would be resting or at the chapel. My mother, as usual, would be busy getting the dinner ready. Nobody needed to tell us to take care. There was no need as I have already mentioned. No harm would come to you apart from the usual scrapes. There was certainly no danger from anyone else, although one day I had my doubts...

A crowd of us were playing with a tennis ball, now grey and tattered with age, bouncing it off the walls as we made our way to McCreesh's for messages for someone or other. Great care had to be taken to ensure our lack of control didn't result in broken windows. Seldom did we break any and if we did all that was required of us was to apologise to the owner, tell our parents and that was that. We were certainly unaware of any offer made by our parents to fix the windows. It was probably made but definitely not accepted. You got an ear full and that was that.

Anyhow we were well on our way, the ball bouncing off the walls with exquisite timing, until someone missed it and through the gate of the local cobbler it went. As it was my turn to next whack the ball it was down to me to retrieve it from its resting place in the corner of the courtyard. I really should have knocked on the half open door and asked could I retrieve the ball but as I heard activity from within the house I decided not to bother. The sun shone brightly as I made my way across the yard to pick up the ball, then I would be off. Simple.

Feeling rather vulnerable in the bright courtyard, almost as if I was alone on a spotlighted stage, the hushed audience awaiting my offerings. I grabbed the ball, somebody grabbed me. I froze.

A harsh angry voice invaded my innocence.

"What are you doing, ye wee scitter, ye?" It was none other than 'Bunk' Toal, a once fearsome sight in the green and yellow jersey of Forkhill gaelic team and now a fearsome sight in his jacket and trousers.

What was I doing? I was shaking. Was the man blind?

He slowly dragged me round so I was facing him full on. His patchy toothed mouth leered at me. "What do you want?" he enquired with a grin on his face which lacked the hallmark of friendship. I couldn't speak, the words weren't even bothering to form in my mind. He continued: "If you say you're nothing but a wee shite, I'll let you go." I hardly let the words rest in my mind let alone say them.

"Go on, say it. Say you're nothing but a wee frigging shite and you can go."

Oh, so he's adding to it, now. A wee frigging shite.

I could hardly look at his saliva foaming mouth as he with a nod of his head urged me to say the words. "Go on, it's dead easy. Just say you're a wee shite and you can take your ball and run. A wee shite, that's all." It might be all to him but to me... the consequences of uttering such terms were dire. He looked at me again as I spied my pals taking furtive glances round the wall and stepping back on realising my predicament. Just as quickly as he grabbed me he released me and give me a kick up the backside and shoved me out.

"You're a wee shite," he called after me.

I thought we had already established that.

My pals surrounded me. "What did he do, what did he do?" Everyone wanted to know as we took to our heels and got as far away as possible, resting finally on an old tree trunk near Dooley's house. I was still recovering from the attack and my normally overworked vocal cords were unable, as yet, to reveal the true circumstances of my imprisonment and subsequent interrogation. More prompting from my pals.

"He wanted me to say I was a wee S-H-I-T-E." Their wide eyes bore down on me as my spelling presented the case. Some weren't sure what I was spelling but were impressed, nevertheless. Others actually spoke the word, a sudden spike in the quiet respectable air of the day. I of course had no difficulty with the spelling, sure didn't my father's typewriter think that was my surname.

"Did you..?" was the next eagerly asked question. Now I was in a bit of a quandary here for to admit to swearing in front of an adult would undoubtedly bring respect from my friends. On the other hand such an admission would find its way back to my mother and, well...

"No, I didn't and I got the ball back as well," I proudly exclaimed. Honour seemed to be satisfied.

"Fucker" someone announced and we all giggled and headed off bouncing the ball once again off the walls. This was pre-TV days so you had to appreciate that certain adults had to get their fun somehow.

Another one to be aware of at times was Paddy Campbell, a brother of 'Hop's and related in the same way to a rarely seen member of the family 'Wings' Campbell. God knows how he got that name. Paddy was a problem especially if he was headed towards McCreesh's shop armed with two big steel buckets overflowing with blackberries. He would get a few shillings for his catch and McCreesh's would sell the sweet berry to jam making mothers. Paddy, as far as I can remember, lived alone, measured to the height of about five foot nothing and was bogging most of the time. His face and hands were jet black regardless of whether he had been picking fruit or not. In his dark black suit he resembled a charred stump of a tree trunk.

An absence of teeth somewhat distorted his speech, that and the porter. After a successful business deal with Sean McCreesh he would adjourn to O'Neill's and imbibe with his new found wealth until he could just about stagger. On his way to the shop he would come over the hill like in the cowboy films holding on to his buckets as if they were guns.

We used to tease him by saying things like "how are you, Paddy?" Innocuous in the sublime, you might think. But Paddy was not a man for social intercourse be it on his way to the pub or coming from it. To see Paddy's reaction to our simple request you'd think we had threatened his life for he would stand up straight, take a deep breath, pucker his lips, the perspiration tripping him.

"Hug, agh, fugh, basts," would be about the formation of sounds from his blackened gob. All this to the accompaniment of flailing arms and blackberry topped buckets. As we watched him meander down the road, the odd gesticulation being chucked back at us, we would wonder what exactly it was Paddy wanted to tell us.

I wonder did he ever realise that we were only asking after his health?

I was to come across many more characters, some similar, many entirely different in my time in this village but for now play was all I was interested in.

Chapter Nine

"Are you coming out to play?"

Words as common as "your dinner's ready" but much more of a kick start to adventure. Meal times were more or less about the same time every day and the menu varied little. But playing... a child going out to play is like letting a big box of multi-coloured balloons free at once. Ideas of what to play flew into the air and scattered in all directions from an overworked imagination. Games.

'Cowboys and Indians; Who could fall the best?; Queenio, Queenio, Who's got the ball?; guider racing; fighting; spitting; football; climbing; Falling down; or just resting against an ole stone wall watching the world go by'. The latter a firm favourite of mine to this day.

When I called for friends we were never sure what we were going to get up to. We had to endure the obligatory chat with the parents before we could be off. All depended on what time of day it was, what the weather was like and how we felt in ourselves. Did we feel just like playing around somebody's house or did we feel like crossing this familiar world and taking a trip down Orney Lonen? There we would be met by monsters jumping out at us from every unruly green trailing hedge. Maybe, however, we'd just stand at a farmer's gate and call his horse down to us, watching its lazy, slightly suspicious trot through the green stained field. The big brown gentle monster would say hello with his massive clear tongue as we pulled our hands away from the velvety organ.

If we were really adventurous we would dander on a bit further to goad a bull. From about three fields back. This put quite a bit of strain on our yet to be fully developed vocal cords to at least catch the animal's attention. If we were lucky he might look up from his grass diet and give us a cursory uninterested glance. We soon ran out of shouts and the bull ran out of what little interest he had in us. Another day. Another day we would get closer. Yeh.

Our favourite game was the universally recognised cowboys and indians. Orney Lonen provided a great arena for the traditional game, as indeed did the back of the barracks.

There was a forced opening linking our house to the barrack field, which was a good couple of acres looking down on the amphitheatre that was the purple stained rhododendron bushes, ever concealing and perfect for our games. Nearby in the station yard sat a rather dejected old rusting shed housing a few lost and seldom claimed bikes. The landrover used to sit back in garage which faced big wooden gates denying entry from outside.

Our sturdy weapons were bits of sticks, making guns for the cowboys, cavalry and the indians. As bows and arrows were in limited supply we changed the historians' tales and had the indians as well armed as the white man. A search round the chickens in somebody's yard might throw up a loose feather for the chief; if not a few chickens had to run for their lives or be scalped. Rest periods allowed us to munch on my father's garden peas freshly popped from their green velvety shields. Captured prisoners found themselves in the shed. It was easier to take prisoners than to keep on shooting everyone for nobody ever admitted to being hit. Oh, aye, you might go through the throes of pain and scream, falling about all over the place, but you resisted the onslaught of death. And then there were the invincible buggers. 'I was behind the bush when you shot', or the unimaginative 'you missed'. It was difficult to argue with being pulled through the bushes and chucked into the shed.

Most of the time we had to shove the old rusty bikes out of the way to make room for our prisoners. However, there were times when we had to find a new venue when the ageing bikes were replaced by a more animated form, namely in the shape of smuggled pigs.

Smuggling was in those days an art form and as natural to the participants as breathing is to the rest of us. And it was a game. Truly.

Illegal it was, to be sure, so therefore not exactly an honest way of making a living, but nonetheless it was a game of chance being played between the smuggler and members of the RUC. The better strategist coming out on top.

Pigs, sugar and butter were items regularly smuggled. Indeed there was a man out Jonesborough way who was quite a keen and indeed experienced smuggler of bags of sugar. He used to engage in his work on dark evenings adorned in a large knee length trench coat, inside of which were pockets galore, willing residences for the pound bags of sugar from which he was going to make a few shillings. If ever he was on a wee jaunt and spied a RUC patrol he would gather up his coat and throw himself, face down into the grassy ditch. It was a bugger if it was a wet night. He would then take on the sounds and movements of a courting couple, the massive mounds in his coat resembling in the fading light a well rounded form normally associated with the fairer sex. The cursory glance from the policeman's torch would not reveal his true mission. Off he went.

Strangely enough, I don't think he ever married.

There was it had to be said a good deal of money to be made from smuggling. A fortune in some cases. Pigs were strong currency. One night my father and a couple of the lads were out near the border hiding behind a thickly covered ditch on the look out for one particular smuggler. This was the fifth night out on what would be called surveillance today. Now this man would have known he was being watched and would have avoided being out and about for a few days. But he had a living to make and had to take a chance on the operation being called off and the police losing interest. Or just getting bloody cold.

The patrol had set themselves up in the ditch just a few yards from the border and watched and waited. Whispered complaints from the freezing and bored young policemen were ignored by my father who was determined to nab this bloke. His luck was in.

Down the Tievecrum Road came the old lorry, lights dead to evade detection. A futile precaution if ever there was one for the lorry creaked and backfired every step of the way and what, with the accompanying swearing from the angry driver, the dead would be wakened never mind a few sleepy policemen. The approaching vehicle was being watched on all sides and as it neared my father flashed his torch giving the signal to his men that the lorry was to be stopped. One of the constables leapt into the road and with a swirling motion of his dazzling torch bade the vehicle to stop. My father and the rest of the patrol emerged from the shadows, groans and grunts spitting out from stiffened limbs. A formidable if somewhat invisible force presented itself to the smuggler.

"HALT," the policeman called. The vehicle spluttered a bit and came slowly to a stop.

"Evening, Sergeant," came the friendly greeting from the driver as he edged his head out the window. EVENING! It was more likely to be a good few hours after midnight.

"Evening, Peter," my father replied, equally friendly. "Mind if we have a wee look in the back of the lorry?"

"Well, to be honest, sergeant, I am in a bit of a hurry, like. Maybe another day, eh?" At this stage of the proceedings voices were having to be raised as the grunting from the back of the lorry had climbed an octave or two.

"Ah, well, I'll have a look anyhow, Peter."

An explosion of grunting, squealing pigs greeted the opening of the back doors.

"Ah, Jaysus, sergeant, watch me frigging pigs."

My father, ever with an eye for an opening said. "Ah, so you admit they are your pigs?"

"Well, not exactly, sergeant..." himself spluttered. "Well the thing is, sergeant..." his voice fell to a whisper and he beckoned my father over to him with a nod as he shoved his glasses back onto his twitching nose. My father moved across. "Don't I know this is wrong, sergeant. Illegal, even. But sure don't I have ten wee pairs of bootees to buy for the little ones and no other means of earning a decent living?" His pleading face shone in the light of my father's torch like a halo. Ten wee bootees for ten wee children. A tragic tale if ever there was one.

My father if he was nothing else was a sympathetic and

understanding man and normally would have been moved to tears by this tale. Only problem was Peter had neither wife nor children.

"I'm taking the pigs" exclaimed my father. Peter, realising he was on to a bit of a loser here, decided to go into action, and jumped out of the lorry to see the policemen begin to unload the pigs and shepherd them towards the landrover amid much grunting and squealing; sounds not exclusively from the animal world.

"Ah, now, sergeant, have a heart. Sure let's see if we could do a bit of a deal here, eh? There's no point in us falling out over a lock of pigs. Sure didn't I see your good lady over by Mullaghbawn and sure didn't we have a chat and get on like a house on fire?" My father stared at him waiting for the offer. "Take five of them skinny ones and two of the fatter. Eh, what do you reckon?"

"All these pigs were smuggled, I'm here to take them all, not just the skinny ones."

A few exasperated groans from the lads as they wanted to be off to bed with or without pigs, skinny or fat.

"Sergeant, you're well known round about these parts as a fair man, so you are. Surely now we can come to some arrangement to suit all parties, eh?" My father had a walk round the pigs who were very well behaved it had to be said, they just nudged about the hedges.

"Switch on your lights 'till I have a better look" ordered my father.

So there you had it. In a South Armagh lane at about two o'clock on a fairly mild morning as the rest of the world dozed in their dreams a mixture of fat and thin pigs parted company with Peter and were taken to the barracks. Off Peter went on his way with a less than full load but not an empty one either. All sides appeared pleased.

And of course there was the social side to smuggling. The Gardaí in Dundalk would on occasion hold a dance to which they would invite the RUC. The place would be coming down with drink kindly supplied by... the smugglers themselves. They didn't actually attend though. Wouldn't be right, would it?

Chapter Ten

School was still the niggling sore it always was. It was about this time that it was presenting us kids with the facts of life, a daunting experience at the best of times but an extremely large burden for us eight-year-olds. What had been rumoured about the playground was in fact turning out to be true.

Yes, we had to stay at school until we were at least sixteen!

Sixteen? I didn't even know what that was or where it was. I had no map to guide me. What I managed to grasp however was that it was a bloody long way off. Not tomorrow, nor the next day, the next month or even a year away. My little mind had no conception of eight years from thence.

Still, there were compensations. We discovered the word 'balls'. Not an earth shattering revelation, you might think, but this word bore no relation at all to the spherical objects commonly used in sporting arenas. Oh, no, this was of a more personal nature.

"How's your balls, boy?" I would enquire of my brother as an early morning greeting.

"Grand, boy, and yours?"

"Never better." I replied as we became engulfed in a fit of the giggles only schoolboys can muster. This was within full hearing distance of our parents and granny. Nevertheless we continued in the same vein for many a morning, the novelty of the same question, answer and reaction not once dampening our pleasure at what we knew and they didn't.

One evening we once again enquired about the condition of

each other's spherical appendages in strong vibrant voices belying the fact that puberty had yet to arrive.

"Now that's enough," my mother suddenly said, a slightly embarrassed look creasing her face. "You're being rude."

Rude?

How did she know we were being rude? Mothers didn't know about these things. How did she even know about the word? Granny continued to eat her dinner, seemingly oblivious to this sudden revelation of adult knowledge which stunned us. Our faces flared up. It was somewhat disconcerting to discover that perhaps we didn't know lots more than our larger versions.

At school we were now coming into the final straight and rounding the bend and facing up to our First Holy Communion. This was a very important time in our young Catholic lives, although tinged with fear, as I have mentioned. A brand new pair of rosary beads encased in a shining white box and your own prayer book were for keeps. More and more school hours were being spent on last minute preparations. Getting ready to be tested by Father McGuinness on our Catechism.

On Wednesdays, however, nothing was allowed to get in the way of our weekly visit to the infants' classroom and our singing lessons with Miss Gaughan. Secure the windows, bolt the doors, tranquillise all neighbouring animals. We lads were about to sing.

Leo's class were in there too. Now for the life of me I couldn't understand why we had to take singing lessons. If you had a talent for something then it is natural and indeed advisable to secure coaching to improve on that god given talent. However this was not the case in the majority of the attendees at Miss Gaughan's weekly soirees. Most of our voices could be used as dubs for nature films; mine in particular was chronic. Our singing lessons were the last class on a Wednesday at about two o'clock when the infants had left the classroom, kindly leaving their own distinctive odours behind. Miss Gaughan was understandably weary after a day teaching. Now she had to guide us along the mined path to dulcet tones.

She formed us into a standing circle around the small room, weird shapes purporting to be drawings of something or other falling from the walls. We lads went to great pains to ensure we stayed well away from the girls as obviously there had to be a link between the sexes somewhere along the line. Misbehaviour at any time resulted in being placed in among the girls while your male colleagues giggled at your red face.

Miss Gaughan had herself a powerful County Louth voice and would start the singing off with her imaginary baton and boom the words out encouraging us to join in with a scowling face and threatening hand gestures. Now the girls were quite happy to sing, many of them had sweet voices and this in itself was helpful to us lads as it enabled our less than melodious offerings to fade, unnoticed, it seemed.

We soon got the hang of this and mimed as the girls sang.

Miss Gaughan soon got the hang of us and would walk around the boys' section, her ear pressed up against our trembling mouths listening to us sing. A courageous stance. She hardly flinched. As soon as she passed each of us we would revert to automatic pilot and mime with an enthusiasm which just fell short of extending our arms embracing the song for all we were worth. She had however this occasional habit of requiring someone to sing solo.

Solo. The very notion struck fear into our hearts. In the main she asked the girls, I suppose she couldn't stand our voices for long. However, one day she had other ideas.

"Shane and Leo White, I would like you to sing together." Together, apart, double sided. Whatever, it made no difference.

The Bonny Bonny Banks of Loch Lomond would never be the same again.

Leo 'took the high road' and I 'took the low...' and Scotland must have been shaking in its boots awaiting 'and I'll be in Scotland afore ye...' Our voices reverberated round the class with the giggles of our classmates more in tune than we were. Now if an animal made this sound you would put it out of its misery. Why not us? Our embarrassment and shaking bodies were there for all to see. At last our kind, considerate, understanding memories came to the rescue.

We forgot the words.

Chapter Eleven

The day of our First Holy Communion was fast approaching. As mentioned before I wasn't a great lover of going to mass. I always felt a bit out of it being unable to receive communion. The words 'Body of Christ' did however have a magical sound to them. I watched the priest open the sacristy and take out the bread, wipe the chalice and drink from it. Holiness abounded. As I watched my family go up to communion I sat spellbound. Either that or stick my tongue out at a friend.

Father McGuinness turned up to test us on our catechism asking a few questions of us. Most of us were shaking in our seats, eyes down. If you can't see him, he can't see you. Your heart missed a beat when a name was called out, relief when it wasn't yours. You were in awe of the priest, having great inherent respect for him. A respect for the cloth was something I was to lose in a few years. Anyway we all passed the first stage, all the questions were answered correctly. Like everyone else I knew the answers off parrot fashion and would have failed to supply the correct one only if nerves had jabbed too much. They didn't.

On the Saturday morning we were to receive our First Holy Communion and the final touches were applied with a visit to the hairdresser's in Newry where my hair was plastered with lacquer making me sleep four inches from the pillow that night. It was a strange time. Exciting, worrying, thrilling.

At about eleven o'clock we all turned up at Mullaghbawn chapel following frantic searches in the early hours for missing veils, socks and, in one case, a suit. All that in the past now as proud parents gossiped with each other, occasionally adjusting their offspring's apparel. We tried to remain as dignified as possible in our strait-jackets of respectable clothing, new suits making us look like cut down adults, ties pushing the top button of our crisp white shirts further and further into our yet to be developed Adam's Apples. The girls stood around giggling nervously in their miniature wedding dresses, a spotlight of warmth following us around all day.

Squint correcting glasses marked a few faces, as did brace filled mouths releasing shy excited smiles. Sticking up hair seemed to be the order of the day as we all trooped into the chapel. It was a pleasant feeling being the centre of attention as we lads took one side of the chapel and our white adorned classmates the other. Parents, to the rear, our teachers close by fussing over us, giving us last minute instructions and smiling nervously themselves. This was an annual pilgrimage for them.

Little of the ceremony remains in my memory as we went through the motions of lining up and kneeling at the altar to receive 'The Body of Christ' in the form of a thin wafer of bread. Tasteless it was. It seemed a lifetime however before we joined our parents outside the chapel amid the sounds of happiness bouncing off the sun soothed morning. Starting to mess about a bit, now we felt a bit more free, we got the odd restraining look but nothing serious. This was our day. Red faces abounded, some from excitement, some from shyness and more than a few as a result of the tight tie effect. The odd Browning camera stuttered into life, allowing a keepsake for generations to come.

Back home I bounded into the house feeling a sense of something special. I couldn't really explain it. I suppose for the first time in my short life I was allowed to feel that bit special, a bit like when you were ill and the whole bottle of Lucozade was yours alone. On a larger scale there was a definite feeling of camaraderie. A sense of something really good. Untarnished.

That and the money from everyone in the village made the day a great one. A fine Irish tradition recognises the first really important step in your life and Mr Kirk was the first to catch me and give me half a crown. I swiftly demolished breakfast and went out in pursuit of my fellow achievers. For once I was happy to stay in my good clothes as they were the identifying label which would secure donations from all and sundry. No matter how little people had they always had something for those having made their First Holy Communion.

This great feeling of togetherness coupled with a pride I suppose I have never really experienced since marked this down as a day to remember. Beaming flushed figures roamed round the village like proud roses saddled to the easy breeze. Small groups of mini-brides and grooms chattered nervously together. Yes, it was a special day.

Chapter Twelve

My father nearly missed the whole show; he was on one of his smuggling trips. Sheep, this time.

This particular smuggler was proving to be the better strategist and had managed to evade detection for many months now. My father only hearing on the grapevine of his successful deeds. One night, a few weeks previously, secure in the fact that this time they would get him, a carefully planned ambush was set up on this particularly lonely country lane for this man was known to have used this road recently. My father and a couple of constables sat behind a ditch waiting for his lorry. It was a wet sort of night and the rain disturbed the calm by tapping their gaberdine overcoats. They hadn't long to wait when the definite utterings of sheep provided an aural delight to the waiting officers of the law.

"Right lads, get ready," said my father confident of nabbing him this time.

A lorry came slowly towards them. Silence descended with the halting of the rain, leaving only the muted breathing of the RUC men and the slow chugging sound of the lorry. Even the stars seemed to hold their breath as they twinkled. The sudden appearance of the local constabulary brought the lorry to a standstill.

"Grand evening, is it not, sergeant?" said yer man, with a feigned look of surprise etched on his rugged features, a prominent nose catching a drip from the roof of the lorry.

"Let's have a look in the back, Michael," said my father. There was little sound now, certainly none of sheep.

"No problem, sergeant, no problem at all." These words cast a little doubt over my father's confidence. One of the lads slowly opened the back of the lorry... nothing!

The familiar sound of sheep suddenly struck a chord though. It was coming from a few hundred yards up the rain glistening road.

"Bugger, this is a bloody dummy run," my father shouted. The sheep were now trickling over the border into safety leaving my father furious and with little option but to wave the man on. The need to get this smuggler was becoming almost painful.

The evening before my First Holy Communion my father and his men were out Jonesborough way, once again laying ambush. It was a bit overcast but they were hiding in the landrover in a side road. A lorry came up the road going like the clappers, its back end nudging the ground.

"A full load," my father announced with pleasure. A constable revved up the jeep and shot straight into the road blocking the oncoming vehicle which would have to stop. The lorry didn't seem to have this in mind and in fact appeared to gain speed. It wasn't going to stop. Ramming the landrover it smashed its way through, a quick glimpse of the driver revealed his now ruddy face opening up into a wide grin.

"After the bugger" roared my father, his cap falling off as he bounced his head against the roof in excitement. The landrover spluttered as it tried to free itself from the clinging grass verge. Nothing but manic spinning wheels. My father threw his hat against the window in exasperation. Giggling constables invaded the chaos for my father wasn't usually given to such outbursts. Suddenly the old vehicle sprang into life, kicking muck all round it, exhaust fumes screaming out. Off they went in pursuit. Determination filled their faces, their prey had no chance.

The empty road for miles caused them unease. Where the hell was the lorry load? Undaunted, these fine enforcers of local law and order drove on eventually arriving at the smuggler's farm. Yer man was there waiting for them, his two big strong sons by his side. With big sneering grins they waited for the long arm of the law.

Unfortunately the long arm wasn't long enough to touch them

for their farmyard was split down the middle – half of it was in the north of Ireland and the other in the south. They were standing in the south giving V signs to the northern police. My father and his men left the scene dejected, seemingly defeated.

The drive back to Forkhill was slow and in complete silence until...

"Wait a minute," my father's excited voice again. "Stop the jeep. We're going back." A smile filled his face as he adjusted his cap strengthening slightly his air of authority. Wonderment filled the rest.

What the smugglers hadn't realised or failed to recognise was that although they were in fact outside the jurisdiction of the RUC the sheep weren't. They had herded the sheep into the north.

Two constables walked the sheep, about fifteen in number, all the way back to Forkhill with my father driving the landrover beeping the odd stray suffering from homesickness.

A victory parade of a good six miles. Once the sheep had been safely deposited among the rusting bikes in the shed the patrol went back to inform their owner what had happened.

They parked the landrover in the yard as the man came out of the house, his face still ablaze with anger. A pitchfork was secured in his hands. My father explained his actions.

"Ye, bastard, ye, Sergeant White," he ranted, his enraged body bulging out of his mud sprouting dungarees, promising all sorts of unusual and complicated deeds with the aid of the pitchfork. The RUC listened to the tirade unwilling to interrupt such a dedicated flow. My father was over six foot and an imposing figure in his black uniform mellowed somewhat by the little disguised twinkle in his eyes.

The smuggler's wife suddenly appeared in the doorway.

"Will ye hol yer whist, Michael, and give me head peace," she said. "Come on in sergeant and have a wee drop in your hand. Bring the lads as well." She gave her husband another disapproving look before slamming the door leaving him there with his thoughts and his pitchfork. My father, never one to miss out on a bit of crack, took his seat by the fire as the men sat by the big kitchen table. In a few minutes the policemen sat with their caps in their laps supping eagerly from hot sweet tea and reaching out for big plates of buttered soda farls, a couple of the farm dogs coming in to welcome the newcomers with wagging tails and open hopeful mouths.

"How's the family, sergeant?" she asked filling up my father's cup, best china for the occasion.

"All grand, thanks. And yours?"

"Well, you can see for yourself, the big gulpin," she laughed nodding in the direction of the yard where her husband once stood. No longer though.

Shuffling sounds from the next room could be heard. What was he doing? Was he getting a gun? Was he really going to threaten them?

He appeared with a bottle in his hand. "If you're going to give these buggers a drink, give them something decent, for god's sake, woman." The bottle of white liquid was opened and glasses filled. Soon the crack was in full swing nicely, aided by the liquid burning the back of their throats.

Poteen, an illegally brewed potion making them the best of friends. Another game over. So my father nearly missed my big day. He looked a bit tired, must have been the crack.

He would have lost a lot more sleep had he known what went on the next day when he detailed a couple of the lads to patrol the local river as poachers were once again on the prowl. Under that old reliable cover of darkness the two policemen went down to the river, one mentioning that he had never actually tasted fresh salmon.

"Have you not?" said the other. "Can't beat it. Would you like some?" A tentative, somewhat bemused nod had the other policeman stripped to the waist, face and hand into the water and with the aid of two sticks and his colleague holding on to his legs, a fresh salmon was secured.

The problem of how to get it into the barracks without my father noticing was overcome by one policeman taking off his waterproof coat and placing the salmon in one sleeve, throwing the coat over his shoulder and holding on to the bottom of the occupied sleeve.

The Salmon was lightly sautéd in butter in the early hours of the morning while my father snored contentedly in his bed safe in the knowledge that law and order was being upheld by his trusty men.

Chapter Thirteen

There were two postmen servicing the area, Johnny Flynn and Herbie Longridge. They were the best of friends and were not averse to taking a few drinks in one of the local hostelries. Johnny lived a few yards from the border and Herbie in the opposite direction, some two or three miles away near the primary school.

Each and every night on which they imbibed they would follow almost the identical routine in order to reach home. Herbie's home being the first port of call and one which required them to pass the police barracks.

"Straighten up, Flynn," Herbie would slur. "We're passing the polis station." The two of them would then make a desperate attempt to locate their upper torsos a respectable degree from their knees. This was done by swaying and saluting towards the barracks and then staggering on. And all without the aid of music.

About half an hour later they would once again appear with Herbie's voice to the fore. "I'm not... not having yous walking home alone." The less than dulcet sounds of the drunk bringing to the attention of whoever was on guard duty the re-emergence of our village postmen. Another bit of swaying and saluting was met with a friendly salute. The two men, arms entwined, would make their way towards Johnny's home which was at the bottom of a steep hill. This went on for hours. It's a wonder we ever got any post the next day. But we did.

Johnny usually did our end of the village stopping outside our house each morning, showing little signs of the night before, and carefully emptied the contents of his sack and then lined up the letters/parcels on our wall in street order. He would then grab a pile and off he would go leaving the remaining post resting happily on the wall. He would be gone a while having a bit of crack or a drop of tea somewhere. People would pass our house, have a shufftie at the mail, retrieve what was their's and go about their business. Nothing was ever stolen.

We were weaned on the milk of honesty. We cared about others and the crime rate in the village was negligible putting aside normal crimes such as smuggling etc! There was only one family whose young lads were known to steal from shops and set fire to things. My father had to have a few words with them on more than one occasion. They were, I suppose, what would be referred to today in this horrendous new mushrooming language as a dysfunctional family. Then, they were a problem family.

Words penning them into a certain section of our society. They were neither a problem family nor dysfunctional. They just had a bastard for a father. He was evil, without a trace of human kindness. He would take a strap to them for no reason at all and beat them unmercifully. His wife was a small timid woman who on his death brightened like a blooming flower and actually smiled. Why wasn't something done to help this family? What were the clergy doing? My mother helped the eldest daughter find a job in Portadown and gave her clothes and shoes. The old bastard burned the shoes.

I once stole one of my granny's digestive biscuits, she used to keep them in a tin box on top of the green dresser in the kitchen. Not purposely out of reach, I don't think, but unavailable nonetheless. I would normally ask if I wanted one and would not be refused, in fact a handful would be pressed into my hand. But there was nobody in the house. Granny was over at Dromintee. I munched happily on a couple and then another couple until only crumbs were left. That and a terrible feeling of guilt.

My guilt was compounded with a sledgehammer when I was out playing and watched my granny being lifted out of a car and being helped up the steps of our house by a priest and another man. Her right leg touched the ground only fleetingly as if the ground was on fire. She had slipped on some wet moss outside the chapel. Her leg was broken. At 79 years of age it was not the best thing to happen to her. And I had eaten all her biscuits. My mother was extremely worried, my father in a state. He idolised her.

She made a full recovery, so much so she had me out with her every night for about a hour walking about the village, her walking stick flicking the tarmac as she strode out. Sometimes I got fed up doing this but as the disappearing biscuits hadn't been mentioned I reckoned I'd been let off lightly.

My granny, on my mother's side, was the only grandparent my brother and I knew. She was lovely, a gentle proud woman. She had worked very hard bringing up three daughters on the family farm at Glasker, near Banbridge. Her two brothers and one sister also lived there with various farm animals including the usual dogs and cats and two goats named Jewel and Biddy who good naturedly in the summer months let the young girls use them as pillows while they dozed in the sleepy afternoons. The girls would bring in the cows for milking, holding on to their tails and twirling them as they sang along the dusty laneways. Now and again the cows got bored and let them have a mouthful of yesterday's dinner straight in the face!

My grandmother as already mentioned was a dab hand at marbles and my brother and I would often have a game with her before going out to play, allowing her to sneak into the dining room and have a drop of Sanatogen wine to which she was partial. She was often offered a drop but didn't always partake, preferring, it seemed, to slug it from the bottle when nobody was around. Perhaps she didn't think it lady-like to be seen drinking; if she could have caught a glance of herself in a mirror, head back, mouth open as the red liquid slid down her throat, she may well have altered her approach to the drink. Still, she enjoyed it, god bless her.

On Saturday evenings I took her out for her walk earlier than usual as I went with my aunt Yola over the border to get cigarettes, which were a lot cheaper than in the North. We were off to Sean McCreesh's shop, he of the main shop in Forkhill. For some reason Sean was always called Joe. He was also the local undertaker and in fact took care of my father's funeral even though we had been away from Forkhill many years at the time of his death. But at times like this you go back to your own and Sean was the obvious choice.

His little hut just across the border was about two miles from our house, a trail of fun and adventure. Often we would watch the frogs leaping across the road having earlier in the year spied on the frogspawn resting gently on top of some watered area, getting ready for their hopping debut in public. The wriggling tadpoles provided great amusement. Spring heralded the snowy hawthorn bushes bowing gently below the horse chestnut trees with their candle-like blooms lighting up their majesty like a Christmas tree. Soon they would provide us with conkers and hours of pleasure. Honeysuckle bushes tickled your nostrils, their sweetness wafting in the air long before the vision of their yellow blooms came into view. The elusive cuckoo teased your vision as you strained to catch a glimpse of this hermit like bird. No amount of climbing trees ever secured a sighting.

The summer allowed blackberry picking along the way if Paddy Campbell had left any, or just watching the bees traipsing from flower to flower amid the multi-coloured butterflies showing off their dazzling clothes.

Winter and its risky slides down Sheen Road as my aunt kept well into the ditch to avoid mishap. Sometimes we'd stop for a while for a chat with Mrs Meaney and her son, Vince, my best friend. On down the steep hill where Johnny and Herbie meandered home.

I was becoming interested in football more and more, preferring soccer to gaelic, and my favourite player was that fantastic Russian goalkeeper, Lev Yashin. I had seen him occasionally on TV pulling off fantastic saves. Better than big Pat, even! There was one shot he saved by diving to the right as the ball shot that way, then took a deflection and flashed across his goal. In mid air Yashin turned full circle and flicked the ball over the bar. I was stunned. I wanted to be a goalkeeper, I wanted to be Lev Yashin. So when I wasn't fighting or admiring nature on the way to Joe's I was twisting in the air like Lev, flicking an imaginary ball over the ditch. People would pass us, stop to talk with my aunt and all the time I was engaging in aerial acrobatics. Nobody took a blind bit of interest. I was playing, I had an unchained imagination. I was a child.

Joe sold cigarettes and sweets, and what a selection of the latter.

His shop was no more than a little old dark wooden cabin resting into the side of the road but it seemed to me to be a different world. Erratic naked light bulbs provided dimmed vision, accentuated by the steady stream of pipe smoke funnelled by a few regulars seated in the corner, eyes glued to the small TV set sitting high up on the wall. Radio Telefis Eireann providing flickering monochrome images. We were greeted by a nod from the regulars and a smile from Joe. A traditional respect was bestowed on my aunt simply because she was a woman. They would mind their language now but our presence in no way diminished the crack bouncing off the walls. A faint smell of alcohol would mingle with the sweetness of tobacco as the chat continued. One or two men would simply listen, pipe in mouth, as if nature selected this spot for them on a Saturday night.

As I am more and more reluctant to cross the door on a Saturday night here in England where I am met in pubs by video screens, loud mouthed drinkers and impatience, I yearn for the calmness and friendliness of Joe's old cabin.

Each Saturday I had only so much to spend on sweets and I looked carefully over Joe's offerings squeezed together in small white boxes resting on the counter. Penny chews, lucky lumps, liquorice snakes with little aniseed beads peeked up at you. These and the old regulars like black jacks contested with dolly mixtures for your few pence.

Sometimes I used to settle for a lucky bag and rip it open to find what mysteries awaited me. A little plastic watch; a dice; or maybe a small toy containing a ball bearing testing your navigational skills as you tried to slot it in holes. If your toy disappointed you there was always the half dozen or so sweets to fall back on.

The journey home, often in pitch darkness or fading light, was less energetic than the outward mission as I had my sweets to spoil my attention. Chewing hard on a bubble gum I would blow a big bubble and listen to the explosion as it burst and covered my face in its pink glue. Struggling with my tongue I tidied up my face and did it again until the flavour took a holiday. A liquorice snake would be sucked in and out like spaghetti, the seeds melting in time leaving the raw flavour to savour.

Next day if the weather was fine we would head off in the car to Warrenpoint. My parents had recently purchased a little grey Austin 40 which my father insisted was not a racing car, much to my mother's disbelief for she managed to get a speed out of it that had yet to be acquainted with the speedometer. Once out on the Dromintee Road my father and the men had set up a road block only to watch this small grey car fly past slightly slowing down but only, it seemed, to wave at the men. My father spun round.

"Did you get the number?" he called watching the car fade away.

"Yes, sergeant" said a young constable with a grin on his face. He proceeded to give the number to my father.

"That's my car. Who the hell... oh, Winnie." He shook his head, raised his eyebrows and tutted.

Warrenpoint, the nearest seaside resort to us, was small and cosy and sold the most wonderful Italian ice cream. Even in winter it was great; sitting overlooking the reckless sea, tearing into a piping hot bag of thick vinegary chips, the rain lashing on the windows as your breath steamed up the car. In the summer the promenade was awash with people taking a dander, watching the clear blue sea at peace with itself, awakening now and then but only ever so slightly.

Forkhill was at it busiest on a Sunday for this was the day we were invaded by our tourists, seeking out the prophecies Hop had to offer or a visit to McGuigan's scrap yard in search of a second hand appliance for an ageing car. I have already spoken of Hop; people used to come from miles to hear their fortunes spilling from a tea cup. She was a stout wee woman and she used to sit on a rumpled armchair, covered in various cushions and blankets by her fireside, reciting her tales. The odd smell of burning wood escaping when her stockinged artificial limb got too close to the embers. I doubt whether there was a great deal of truth in what she said, but what her clients did get was a bit of crack for she was a great storyteller. And all for a few shillings. As payment was left to the individual there were a few who did not leave anything. I don't recall ever seeing an unhappy face coming out of Hop's.

McGuigan's scrap yard was the other Sunday alternative. Broken down cars used to stretch up the mountains, literally hundreds of them in various stages of disrepair. It was a bit like Mount Rushmore. Instead of presidents, hub caps and headlamps etched the landscape.

Chapter Fourteen

Holidays were something very few of the locals ever had. We were fortunate in that nearly every year we would head off somewhere. Once to a small caravan in Arklow where bunk beds, no toilets and even less water awaited us. A regular feature of the day was carrying massive buckets of water from the nearest pump.

The Vale of Avoca, a beautiful scenic area surrounded by leafy forests, is where three rivers collide and become one, 'The meeting of the waters' as it is known. Many years later as an adult I returned there and enjoyed a couple of pints with my father in a pub close by. The postman arrived clutching the mail and sat on a stool as a pint of the black stuff was poured for him. Contentedness oozed from him as he sampled the creamy top.

We left Forkhill on the Monday morning to go to Arklow. Once again my father nearly didn't make it.

On the Sunday the landlady of a local pub was having a bit of difficulty removing certain customers from the premises. The fact that she shouldn't be open at all on a Sunday is neither here nor there. She wanted to go to a dance in Dundalk and unless she got these men out she would miss it. A thought suddenly struck her. I'll ring the barracks and complain that there's drinking going on here.

So with a disguised voice she made her complaint and within about an hour my father and one of his trusty constables arrived on the premises to be met with the gentle tinkling of glasses and the roar of conversation. And herself standing there, a look of contentment on her face.

"We've had a complaint about you serving drinks" my father said to the landlady who just held her hands up. At least now, I'll get off to the dance, she thought.

This was about five o'clock. At a quarter to nine my father, the young constable and the imbibers left the premises, the best of friends. My father's ears burning no doubt as herself left him in no doubt how she felt. "I could have got them out meself a hell of lot quicker" she roared, slamming the door behind them and missing the dance.

Coming home from holidays was always great as long as there was still a long time before going back to school. I had to catch up with Colum McConville, the comic swapper, to see what a week away had left me with. I gathered up my offerings to swap and made for his house. I had quite a bit to offer: The Hotspur; Beanos; a Dandy. And all Colum could offer me in return were a couple of Judy's and part of another girl's comic featuring The Three Marys. No thanks. I went back home and re-read about the antics of Ronnie Briggs, my goalkeeping hero. He looked like Harry Gregg and nothing got past him.

My brother had passed the Eleven-plus and would soon be on his way for his first term at St Coleman's College. It was no surprise that he passed for he was intelligent and hardworking. The Eleven-Plus was my next big step in life. The new intelligence test had been introduced and replaced the traditional exam whereby you were tested in English and Maths. Now it was to be a series of short tests designed apparently to test the mental reflexes of we eleven year olds. I had moved up to Master Keating's class and we also moved house. The present sergeant in the RUC House was being transferred and it was decided not to replace him. John Thornton and Margaret Shannon, recently married, moved into our old house.

Our new home was much bigger than the terraced house. I would no longer feel uneasy playing football up the back field for it seemed that the sergeant's wife was not overly happy with us playing in the field. I suppose our dirty football hitting her washing didn't help. We moved in with the minimum of fuss.

I was now able to watch my father drill the lads in the backyard of the station.

"Right, left, right left" he would roar. It was strange to hear him shout. And even stranger to see the lads obey him. But they did. For some reason I was amazed at the power he had. Fortunately for all concerned this practice parade didn't happen very often, usually only when some dignitary was due to visit. Like the Chief Constable of the RUC. The higher echelons of the RUC occasionally deemed it necessary to visit the troops in the 'bog stations'. Helped morale, or so they thought. I don't think anyone was fooled, least of all the young constables who had to endure these parade sessions with my father.

About three months into our new home Mr Kirk took ill. Although we were no longer next door to him we still used to do his messages. The ambulance rushed him off to hospital and in a few days he lapsed into unconsciousness and never came round. We went to his funeral. We weren't long back home when we saw a couple of cars pulling up outside his house. We recognised them from the funeral but prior to that had never set eyes on them. In no time at all chairs, tables, lamps, anything it seemed which wasn't nailed down began to leave the house. They were violating his memory. A while after they had gone we went into the house.

The front door lay open. I half expected to see Mr Kirk sitting in his front room with his arm resting on the unclothed brown table with a cigarette in one hand and his usual cup of very sweet tea in the other. There was nothing there, save silence. A graveyard silence. And these people didn't see fit to honour it.

For us things were changing rapidly, particularly for my mother. She was now becoming more and more active in the community. Somehow or other she had been roped into doing the library on a Thursday night in the old Tech. I was her assistant. In the winter months we would go down a bit earlier than usual to get a good fire on and while it was taking hold I would nip up to Murphy's and get some crisps and sweets. There was a fairly wide range of books on display but you had the regulars who never veered from their recognised preferences. Mrs Morrow and her romantic books; Mrs Gibson and her cowboy books and the odd thriller lover searching the dusty shelves for another enticing episode.

It was my job to date-stamp the books in between stuffing my face. On other nights a Mr Smith from Dundalk would take either cookery or care maintenance classes. The library had a permanent musty flavour and the darkened glass added to the cosiness of the place, particularly in the snow laden nights of winter.

There was one particular bad winter when the snow came and stayed with a vengeance. But we struggled through the elements and got to the library to be met with a few brave, but amazed, people when they saw we had made it.

"Never thought you would make it, Mrs White" one old lady said. It was a bitter night, no mistaking. Soon, though, the fire sprang into life, the crack was in full swing. The difficult weather conditions bringing us together. Us against the elements. There was a sense of community about, a sense of belonging.

The next day however a couple of old dears who hadn't bothered to turn up the night before thinking the library wouldn't be open complained bitterly to my mother.

"Well, we didn't think you would be out so we didn't go. We think it only right that you open tonight for those of us who didn't make it last night." The answer, as I recall it, was, no. A dignified one, at that.

My mother was now responsible for collecting the parish dues, which required traipsing round the village getting people to fork out for the upkeep of our priests. All the time while Rome basked in the obscenity of riches beyond belief. She also would provide a taxi service to hospital in Newry for any injured villagers as well as carting Lizzie Sleith, Mrs Murphy and my grandmother to mass every morning. We were now truly part of the community despite the initial traditional suspicion. My father, after all, was in the uniform of the RUC.

Chapter Fifteen

On a calm sunny evening the IRA machine-gunned the ill prepared RUC station at Crossmaglen, the attack lasting about twenty minutes. Young inexperienced policemen finally faced the enemy firing sterling sub machine guns and M1 Carbines in response to the spluttering Thompson machine guns. The Thompson, in time to be referred to as 'The Widow Maker', following its success at the beginning of the troubles.

A report from Newry barracks was that we were next.

Was this just a re-emergence of IRA activity for no apparent reason other than the usual periodic onslaught as though they wanted to keep their hands in? The IRA then were not particularly well trained or indeed armed. Nor young. Nor experienced. Nor overly dedicated to any cause.

Not like today.

My father was left with the decision as to whether he should alert the whole village, risking mass panic. As usual he discussed it with my mother; he was after all a young inexperienced policeman as well. Sitting on their bed facing the street they decided the best thing to do would be to alert the people in the houses nearby. If the IRA came they would fly past the barracks shooting and the risk of any civilian houses being hit was remote. My brother and I, unaware of what was happening, wanted to go out. As any child whose home was about to be machine-gunned would!

When we were told what was happening we weren't frightened, just excited.

The early evening took on a still, remote caress. A waiting game. The rusty steel shutters were dragged screeching into place. Our bedroom window didn't have any and we faced the road they would travel from Crossmaglen. It was envisaged they would travel through Silverbridge, down the twisting Beardies and fly through the village opening fire on the barracks and then make good their escape by speeding down the steep hill to Larkin's pub and up the Carricksticken Road. In a few miles they would be in the South. And safety. My father radioed Newry barracks asking for the promised reinforcements.

They never came. Bog station.

There was a peep hole in each of the shutters to allow slight vision and the tip of a gun. My father stood with a sterling cradled in his arms looking out through his bedroom window. It was a strange sight, seeing my father with a gun.

"Time you were off to bed" he said smiling gently at me. This wasn't my father, was it? This man with a gun. I was suddenly frightened.

A young Derry lad with cherubic features stood at our bedroom window as Leo and I got into bed, giggling. A child's adaptability allowed me once again to laugh. The young lad's gun scanned the road. A slight tremor in his hands. A road which earlier had been stained with children's' laughter. My mother was at my father's side, despite him telling her to go downstairs. She sat calmly on the bed as he stood seeking, with a sterling, what he hoped would never come.

The creeping, coy darkness was going to throw up many heart stopping shadows.

In the advancing darkness I felt uneasy. There was a quietness which I will never forget. All along Forkhill had been fun. Sandbags at the front of the station a reminder, albeit a dim one, of what could happen. But that was all. Now something was happening. I wanted to go out, to be with my friends. Longing to hear laughter.

I wanted my Forkhill back.

A few cars passed. Nothing. Sighs filling the barracks.

Suddenly a car edged its way towards the station, slowly coming to a halt. There were apparently three gunmen and a driver.

The fading light made it difficult to see who was in the car but nonetheless fingers gently caressed triggers. By now both my brother and I were asleep.

This was for real, this wasn't the firing range at Banbridge where my father hit nearly everything but the target. He hated guns. He often said what use would he have of a gun?

The gunman smiled at my mother before he jumped into the revving car.

RUC guns trailed the car, ready to kill. For the first time.

The car? It sped off into the quiet concealing night. For some reason I woke up then to see the young policeman's hands shake uncontrollably as his grip on his gun eased and his deep sigh echoed round the room.

"Sorry, did I wake you?" he asked. I shook my head. This young lad should have been out with his girlfriend somewhere or maybe just chasing smugglers.

The night strolled along peacefully. The car that passed? It did indeed contain the IRA unit. Why they didn't open fire, nobody knows. The unrelenting, savage, screaming voice of terror which would soon scar our country in years to come was then but an embryo.

Oh for abortion.

Chapter Sixteen

A couple of days later after school I called into the barracks to find one of the constables with a bruised and battered face. Did something happen that night that was being shielded from me? I was to hear the truth from the giggling voices of his colleagues.

Things had returned to normal following the scare and as usual the lads were out on patrol again. Smuggling time again. The IRA would have to wait.

The injured policeman it transpired had been watching with binoculars as a lorry came over the Beardies Hill, approaching the concealed patrol, slowly and deliberately. This particular constable leapt out of the ditch as the lorry got nearer to apprehend the suspected villain. A bit early as it turned out. The driver jumped out of the vehicle, raced to the back of his lorry and with the agility of a man whose arse was on fire swung open the heavy doors.

"Get out, get out, shoo, shoo" he roared at the piglets and they swiftly responded to the command and squealed their way towards the border and safety.

The binoculared policeman took a leap in the air and off he went after the pigs, the remainder of the patrol, including my father, watched with a mixture of admiration and with a notion to recommend psychiatric treatment to their colleague.

"Come back, ye bastards" he cried as he took off down the road. A request which would be met with a basic refusal from your ordinary human law breaker was met with complete indifference from the piglets. These trainee pigs infuriated the constable as he watched his prey making great strides towards the muddy banks of the Republic of Ireland. Up the grassy fields he ran, successfully encountering an extremely muddy patch and up an over a ditch. A few thorns joined his body round about this time and round about his arse. An impressive sight as you can imagine. He was almost within touching distance of the border as his hand stretched to grab a few piglets. Unfortunately, this last and decidedly impressive attempt to catch the livestock had resulted in his binoculars smashing off his face for the last few minutes with every gasping stride he took. He was knocked almost unconscious and after the final thump fell to the ground, a squealing piglet held firmly by its spindly pink tail. He almost had his eyes put out.

A tired and triumphant member of Her Majesty's Royal Ulster Constabulary lay covered in mud. Winking. Out of his good eye.

Although the time to take the dreaded and totally unwelcome Eleven-Plus was fast approaching, life was still great. Our amusement was still mainly in our own hands and sometimes we had real treats, things which I would think kids of today would take for granted or even sneer at.

The nearest cinema was in Dundalk and the school would sometimes arrange to go and see a film. Liberty Valance was the first film I ever saw on the big screen. Another lesser known film preceded the main event. There's a lovely Belfast expression describing somebody who is a bit too big for their boots: 'He thinks he's yer man in the big picture'. Before entering the cinema we would sample the delights of a big bag of chips, costing sixpence, setting us up for an enjoyable evening. Pure heaven.

On other occasions a trip to Dublin was organised, usually in the summer holidays. A bus took us from just over the border in Kilkurry to the railway station in Dundalk for the onward journey to the capital by train. All of us would walk from the village to catch the bus as a lovely blanket of warmth opened the day, escorting giggling, excited children and their parents. Wee brown paper bags packed with sandwiches were clutched in our chubby hands.

We were off to Dublin. Parentless. Teachers now looking after us.

None of us had ever been on a train before and as it puffed nonchalantly out of Dundalk, proving a load of school children wasn't a problem to this seasoned voyager, we all ripped open our paper bags and devoured our lunches. Excitement digging big holes in our stomachs.

There were a couple of children whose parents couldn't afford the fares so Master Keating paid for them out of his own pocket, as he did another time when we were held spellbound when a magician visited our school and pulled pennies from behind our ears. It was like that then.

Those were the really special times but in between we had the gift and imagination of our young minds to keep us amused every day. And fire was to prove attractive. We were of course not allowed to play with matches and light fires because of obvious parental concerns. It was therefore difficult to obtain matches unless you confessed to smoking seventy a day or needed your pipe refilled. Not to be recommended really. But somehow or other one of us would manage to steal a match or two from home. Armed with the end of a matchbox we would amble up the fields and start a fire with sticks and bits of any old wood we could find.

In no time we would have a strong fire going and our smiling contented blackened faces were soon gazing into the spiralling flames as they stretched wearily for the skies. We were full of amazement at this small miracle. But it was time to do a bit of roasting – I use this word loosely – and spuds were our victims. We would dig them up and chuck them unwashed into the blazing fire and move them about every now again with a stick to ensure an all over cooked look. Rescuing them after a few minutes having decided they were about done we studied their outward appearance as we skewered them on to thin pieces of wood. Beautiful. From the outside.

The innards were rock hard and very, very hot. But by god did they taste good.

When we arrived home following our picnics we would have blackened faces, hands, and maybe the odd sleeve or two of your jumper would reveal a big brown singed mark.

"You've been lighting fires again, haven't you?" our mothers would scold.

"Haven't, mum, honest" came our innocent offering. I think all we thought we needed to do to fool our parents was to look innocent and deny everything. It was as if only young eyes could see the state of us.

Another favourite pastime was a game we called 'who could fall the best?' which involved siting ourselves at the top of some grassy bank. One person would be situated further down the hill. Girls wouldn't play this game as it involved a lot of rolling about and they were slightly reluctant, well most of them, to reveal their underwear despite not infrequent requests to do so. You learned at an early age girls were little fun. I'm not entirely sure what our fascination with girls' knickers were at this time in our lives for in general they resembled threadbare blankets of varying colours and indeed shapes.

Anyhow our game progressed with the lad at the bottom shooting at the advancing party of Indians with a stick. We would all fall mortally wounded, breathing our last, uttering final words which no doubt would have found favour with the Cherokee or Comanche tribes as they carried out their war dances. Gymnastic variations littered the area as we strove to be marked highly for our presentation and authenticity as we were grabbed by the throes of death.

One hell of an advantage at this stage was if you met with a clatter of nettles on your tumble down, for your shouting and gesticulations would win you an Oscar.

Night time never seemed to be in any hurry in those days, the day seemed to stretch its sunlight for longer than the allocated amount. We, however, loved the darkness. The cold closing in evenings allowed us the opportunity to display our manly protective talents. We formed a patrol to protect the good people of the village, realising that my father and his men had enough on their plates.

If my memory serves me right this gallant group was made up of: Myself; Leo; John and Colum McConville; Sean (Pudger) Judge, my best friend; and Martin Thornton who was my best friend at one time but got fed up hanging around at the wall opposite our house watching the world go by. A wall at which I tried to stand when I returned to Forkhill for the first time, six months after we had left to go to Newry.

"Fuck off, mate" came the voice of a soldier as I looked up at what was once my home. God, how times had changed.

Dressed in our heaviest coats, some belonging to our fathers, and trailing the ground extensively within a six mile radius, carrying toy guns or just big thick sticks, we would dander around the village, ever vigilant, ever conscious of the need to protect our people. Sometimes our stealthy advances were interrupted by somebody pricking themselves on the blackthorn 'gun' they were carrying.

"Shush" we would whisper in unison. He in question would sulk and threaten to go home. We advanced nevertheless.

We would meet people out for a stroll or off down the pub. Safe as houses they were but they put up with us stopping them and asking them where they were going and what they were doing? Most laughed, and to their credit nobody told us to piss off. That was a good sign, maybe we were being accepted by the people as a force with which to be reckoned.

After about a week we were really into it and had organised ourselves into groups of two. I was with Pudger. The highlight for us was one evening when the old watchmaker from just over the border came swaying down the road after a few hours in the pub, his long dirty coat covering his large skinny frame and more often than not catching in the wheels of his creaking bike.

We would stand in the middle of the road, careful not to fall on our faces as our coats pulled on our legs nearly every step of the way.

"HALT."

To his credit he never failed to stop. Probably thought we were the police. Porter can play tricks on the mind. Most of a very pleasant nature, thank god. He would chat to us, well slur at us really. He would tell us about his watchmaking days, which appeared to be in the past somewhat. We would cod him on about him visiting a certain local woman who was considered as being available, so to speak, for a few shillings. We weren't absolutely sure what this meant but we did know it had something to do with 'sex'. And we knew more about it than a lot give us credit for. Although it was never discussed with adults. What did they know about it?

Now we knew what cows and bulls got up to. And they usually got up to it in the field right beside us as we passed the time of night with him. This was the beginning of our sex education. He told us he had only been visiting her to fix her clock.

Ah, right. We assimilated this knowledge and had this sex lark figured out.

One had to fear therefore for the safety of any woman who ventured alone into this field with a dismantled clock.

One night we were patrolling near a row of garages which backed on to Haughey's fields. We suddenly heard movement. Moving a safe distance back we listened, our heads turning this way and that as we strained for sound. The mounds of unused overcoat clasped in our hands ready for a quick get away.

"We should have a look" someone offered. The rest of us looked at him. Was he deaf? Did he not realise that there might be some-body or something there? Ready to pounce.

We investigated by both aural and visual means as we continued to move as far away as was honourable. To our credit we retreated slowly. The noise continued. Louder. We continued on our well rehearsed route, ie, as far away from an area resembling trouble as possible. Our exit from the area continued. As we reached the stage where we need fear for our safety only if lurking in those fields was a dinosaur revving up Concorde someone mumbled with a degree of authority. "I'm sure there's something there, we really should go back." Somebody else felt a surge of bravery: "Come on lads, there's nothing to be frightened of, we're all together."

Jesus, what book was he reading? These suggestions might have brought some positive response had the rest of us not scattered in various directions just as they spoke.

"I don't think there was anything" I shouted in a masterful voice as I ran down the road.

"Neither do I" or "You're right." Voices in agreement. We were very brave when it came to agreeing. We disbanded the patrol there and then.

Chapter Seventeen

I failed my Eleven-Plus. I was devastated. My life was finished, who would want a failure? I could offer nothing. I was ashamed to face the village. I was eleven. If my mind had any problem with the reality of the situation my body had no such qualms and threw me into a horrendous asthma attack. Something from which I had never suffered and thankfully never again since. But imagine the trauma which would bring on something like that. I sobbed when I could get my breath in my parents' bed as they showed me the piece of paper condemning me. I thought the day I found out Santa Claus was a fraud was the worst day of life; I was wrong.

Everyone in the village thought I would pass, myself and Billy Guiney. Billy did. There was a flu epidemic that year and I fell victim to it but still sat the exam having been doused liberally with hot whiskeys. The stuff tasted rotten. Shows how ill I was!

My parents, god bless them, said I could still go to St Coleman's College although they would have to pay my fees. I had passed their entrance exam, something you had to do regardless of your Eleven-Plus results. Although I was obviously deeply upset, at least I was still going to follow in my brother's footsteps and go to the College and if I did well enough in my first year I would pass the 'Review' and be awarded a scholarship. I would then be like everyone else. I would not have to pay my bus fare, everyone else had passes. Even those who like me had failed the exam went to Newry Technical college and had bus passes. I hated having to go up to the driver everyday to have my ticket clipped. Nobody said anything to me but I felt it.

At the end of the year all was well and for the start of the new term I would have my pass. I hated school. I just could not master why once again fear littered the classrooms. What part does fear play in the intake of knowledge?

I'll never forget my first day. I was resplendent looking in my new blue blazer and acres too big trousers. I followed Leo on the short bus trip to the College. A number of us 'scaldies' were sitting nervously on the bus twiddling with our school bags, the nauseous smell of leather making some of us ill while the bigger lads smoked and swore at the back of the bus, laughing at us. We all looked so clean and so very frightened. Little frightened faces glistening in the September sunlight.

St Coleman's College sat with a degree of majesty down a long shrub laden drive. The first thing which met your glance was the tall blue and white goal posts nestling in the playing fields in the valley just down from the big red bricked school building. The whole front area of the school was lashed with excited or petrified kids. The boarders had been there a day already. I felt this cold, cold feeling filling my full stomach, my mother having insisted on us having a fry up that morning. The boarders looked more worried than I did. Soon I was to learn why.

I already knew what absolute bastards some of the priests were, and indeed some of the lay teachers, from my brother's tales. Tales which never reached the ears of parents as it was accepted that your teachers had the right to chastise you. Just like your parents had.

If you told your parents you had been caned at school they would more than likely think you had deserved it. As I write there is a current thinking that parents should not be allowed to slap their children. If only a similar outlook had prevailed with regard to the role of our teachers in discipline.

My first day passed in a blur; so many children, so many teachers. Some of the latter smiled at you, others glared at you. Forgetting we were human beings and taking, it seemed, great delight in the fact you were terrified. My brother soon had to leave me but I soon teamed up with a lad from Dromintee, Patsy Boyle, who had this large quiff in his fair hair which all through his school days seemed to remain rigid.

Travelling home to Forkhill that afternoon I was exhausted, every inch of the journey taking me nearer my sanctuary. Nerves tore at my consciousness all day. Never mind, after dinner I was off to Mullaghbawn with my father who had to look into a bit of an argument with neighbouring farmers.

Although technically my father was off duty he nevertheless decided to step in where there was trouble, more for the crack than through a sense of duty, mind you. Dressed in his civilian clothes we entered the farmyard of one of the duelling families. A warm greeting was there for us.

"Come on in, sergeant. Wait 'till we tell you the crack. Is this the youngest?" the woman of the house asked. My father nodded and I smiled shyly. The farmer nodded at us from his chair by the fire. We sat on hard chairs in the unadorned farmhouse kitchen inhaling the beautiful aromatic charms of griddled bread. On the table, piping hot, were plates of newly baked wheaten and treacle bread just waiting be to be buttered.

Soon we were stuffing our faces with the woman's wares as she looked on pleased with how much we were managing to eat. During the day my father had visited the other family and had got their side of the story. As usual, a row over land.

"The thing is, sergeant, them'ns have always been trouble. Ever since we knew them." My father listened as he sipped slowly from a glass of stout, mentally recalling how he had heard the exact same story earlier on that day. "Himself there..." she continued, pointing to her pipe smoking and nodding spouse. "All he was trying to do was to reason with yer man, to tell him not to allow his cattle to graze on our land."

"Ah, you see, there we have the problem," said my father draining the last drops from the glass and watching it fill up again. "He says it's his land." A mischievous glint appeared in my father's eyes on realising that there could be a good bit of crack here.

"And he would," came the voice of the husband, a voice as gentle and warming as the kitchen fire tickling the room. "That's because he's the biggest heuring bastard yer ever likely to meet in this country." His wife nodded enthusiastically as he continued to blow calm misshapen spirals of smoke into the air.

91

"Yes, well, did it really necessitate throwing rocks over the hedge at him?" my father was quick to ask, while accepting another bottle of stout.

"That gobshite, he started it. The state of him too, walking about, arse in pockets," replied the pipe smoker in his defence.

"That's the truth, so it is, sergeant. As sure as me and Jimmy here are sitting talking to you," she said heaving her more than ample bosom up in an apparent act of solidarity.

The story which emerged was that the two farmers, on either side of this rather large ditch, unable to see each other, started to throw stones and rocks in the vicinity of each other. One would let a scream out pretending he was hurt to hear the other proclaiming his accuracy.

"Got ye, ye big shite." The gloating giving away his position. A rock sailed over. Thud.

"Ye fucker, ye, that was my head."

"Spot on then, ye ole bastard." And so it continued.

Nobody was getting anywhere, least of all the innocent cattle, looking on somewhat bemused and aloof as only cows can. Some onlooker saw fit to call the police. Then the accusations started.

Who was right? Who was wrong?

Roughly translated: Who was the bigger liar?

My father, as usual, weighed up the problem, albeit with the assistance of the creamy black stuff. Fortunately the participants in this country màlee had during the day imbibed themselves and a compromise was reached to allow the cattle to cross the fields at certain times.

I can't tell you how long this particular compromise stayed in place. But how long does it take to sober up?

Chapter Eighteen

Everything seemed to be happening to me over the next year or so. I was now at secondary school, playing gaelic for Forkhill and St Coleman's and wishing I was playing soccer. Parading my skills at Windsor Park – Wembley was not yet in my sights – was my preferred dream to playing at Croke Park in a gaelic final.

I never left the house without a football. I dreamed of playing for Manchester United alongside Bestie, Denis Law and Bobby Charlton. I would spend hours in our back yard kicking the ball against the wall.

And then I saw her.

Skinny, trailing blonde hair hanging in the wind as if in a trance. I was in love although I had no idea how to be, what it was or if I had the correct map to follow. Somebody mentioned she was someone else's girlfriend. I was devastated. I had only found her yet someone had got up earlier. I had known her for ages, like a lot of the local girls. The day before I hadn't noticed her.

But today?

It was so sudden, like a flash of lightning. I was going to marry her, no doubt. I still played football. Hey, I had only just discovered girls; I owed my allegiance to it. Why was my heart pumping so hard? There were no iced buns in sight, no plates of finger scorching chips laced with revitalising vinegar. Was I sick? Would I ever recover?

I cannot recall how our eyes met, it certainly wasn't across a crowded room. I wouldn't have dared be in a room with her. I think my pals and her's joined in a game of hopscotch. As we watched the girls delicately touched the surface as they jumped from square to square. We lads decided that the tar hadn't properly set on the road so we proceeded to apply our seemingly size tens with all the finesse of a deranged mountain goat.

She seemed to throw glances my way. I seemed to catch them returning, them all polished and shining. We talked. What about?

Hey, now a bloke needs a degree of privacy in his life, things that only he should know about. Okay, we talked about the fact that we were being called in for our tea.

Tea? Bloody tea? I didn't want tea. My life was about to reach for another planet and I was being offered tea. I went in anyway as she had to go get her's. On a broader scale she was to become a welcome diversion to school as my fears were proving to be all I thought they would be and worse.

In addition however there was always another member of the opposite sex, and she was.

One night a few of us were wandering up the Back Road with nothing particular in mind when we heard the voices of two girls approaching. One of them being herself. We were about thirteen years of age, they about seventeen, I think.

"Spread out lads" someone said. We were going to ambush them and sort of interfere with them, so to speak. With their permission, of course. Oh, we had a degree of subtlety.

So there you had it. Six young lusty lads with the charm and finesse of one of Haughey's bulls during the mating season. We blocked the road, they wouldn't pass. Our chats with the watchmaker would stand us in good stead. The girls were giggling. Good sign. They were getting closer, we tensed.

They walked straight passed us without a glance.

It seemed an eternity before somebody spoke.

"Why didn't you stop them?" was the first accusation.

"Why didn't you?" was the angry reply. "You were nearer."

"Let's play football," was the next comment.

It was pitch black, we had no ball. But it seemed a bloody good idea.

Chapter Nineteen

There were a handful of fairly decent teachers at St Coleman's, but there seemed to be even more evil sods. The priests were undoubtedly the worst. As at primary school these people seemed to feel that a link with fear was an essential ingredient in teaching.

These guys of the cloth, they were professionals. Many of the lay teachers were little better. Our maths teacher, a big thick Southern Irishman, had this habit of suddenly insisting that all our geometry sets be complete, nothing missing. He would give us a week to get things arranged for invariably all of us had some bit or other missing. So all of us scampered about persuading our parents that we needed a new this or that.

The following week we all sat with our bulging geometry cases on display. He never even looked at them. Not that week, nor the following. A couple of weeks later he came bounding into the classroom, cane already drawn.

"Right, let's see you geometry sets."

Shit!

Of course by this time we had all lost bits. He caned everyone of us. A class was spent caning us. And enjoying it.

One particular priest we had was the most evil looking gulpin it could be your misfortune to land your eyes on. A real thick ignorant git. He taught Latin and would for no reason hit you with whatever was handy. He once had a stand up fight with one of the boarders who went to the rescue of a young boarder this priest was laying into. The boarder got expelled.

The priest? Last I heard of him he was a parish priest some-where. Obviously got promotion. Another priest was not happy until he drew blood and would continue until he did; usually this necessitated twelve slaps. Nobody seemed to think there was any-thing wrong with this apart from us kids.

If you were good at sports, as I was, then things were a bit easier for you. If you weren't... then things could be hell. Our lay PE teacher would lash out at those of us who were no good at football using anything from an old guttee to a nail splintered stick. All this for not being able to kick a ball straight or be able to do some physical exercise. It was so humiliating for the victim. Red faces endured the snide remarks imposed by this failure of a human being.

I was very good at football and obviously did not get caned often as they would not want to damage my hands. I was frigging useless at Latin but I didn't get singled out and abused for that failing.

There was however one particular gentle priest who tried to chastise us but we ignored him. We were young lads and only too willing to play on weakness. There should have been a happy medium though.

Bullying was rife and seemingly accepted by the authorities as part and parcel of growing up. Bollocks. Bullying is simply the act of a coward.

Many a fight took place in the handball allies, the boarders in particular being the main combatants. It was probably a build up of pressure, like being in prison, really. I can't imagine prison being much worse. The food here was disgusting. The boarders used to buy food from us day-boys. The cups of thick pea soup I used to dole out were devoured with great gusto. Parents used to pay to have their child boarded thinking they would receive a better education; or simply to get rid of their offspring for most of the year. In my opinion it takes a hard sort to let their child leave, crying from their home, and place them into a world full of the unknown. You must remember here that the majority of parents would themselves have been taught by either priests/nuns or Christian Brothers. They were therefore fully aware of the violence dished out by this lot yet still sent their sons off into the fray. I would much rather my child had little education and a happy childhood for an unhappy childhood never leaves you.

I dare say there are those who would argue with my opinions; so be it. I never really suffered at the hands of these people, I therefore have no personal axe to grind. My only personal regret is that I sat back and allowed my classmates to be treated the way they were. I would not now stand for such abuse of young children.

As teachers the majority were very good, they just failed abysmally as human beings. They were extremely thorough and had a genuine interest, believe it or not, in you getting on. It was difficult to try and reason why this other side came to the fore so often. And then there were the nuns, the horror stories about them. How these people were ever allowed near children I will never know. Perhaps this was the only arena in which they felt they would stand out as individuals. One where we kids would have done anything to please them really but they saw this eagerness as a weakness.

Still there was always home, the weekend and holidays.

Then my brother got expelled. For breaking a window. Something he didn't do but they were determined to get him and his mate out, for they rebelled. Refused to accept the beatings and knuckle under. The President of the College took great delight in expelling them. He died a few years ago and the platitudes in the Newry Reporter made me laugh. He was a moron, was one of the worst teachers ever, couldn't stand the pupils. Not much of a priest either, as you can imagine. I don't know why it is felt that one could well be damned for life should one have the temerity to speak the truth about a man of the cloth. They are like us, human beings. Unlike us, they purport to represent God. He must be a bit of a bugger then!

These so called men of the cloth are now in the main preaching their gospels around Ireland; many of their parishioners have no idea what they did to young, and in the main, innocent boys. They were violent towards a lot of my classmates. And now we have a very violent society in Ireland. Violence breeds violence; these priests played their parts in forming future generations. Well done, Fathers!

These days were not entirely unhappy but any day actually spent at school was. As I say I suffered little but I saw the fear and the abuse often. Maybe others didn't take it so personally. Who knows?

Chapter Twenty

I think it was the Labour Home Secretary, James Callaghan, who sent the troops on to the streets of my country. Callaghan is alleged to have told Gerry Fitt it would be no problem getting them on to the streets but he couldn't feel so confident in getting them off as quickly.

How could this man be the prophet of such a tragedy which would unfolded over the coming years?

The soldiers came to Forkhill; friendly, unconcerned lads. The sleeping arrangements were less than adequate with many snoozing under the kitchen sink and in the bathrooms. Unmarked tins of food led them to eating cocktails of bully beef and peaches with remarkable resilience and appetite. God, we had no idea how long it would last.

Soldiers on our streets meant little to us apart from the obvious novelty value. Their appearance then smacking more of the unprofessional UDR. They seemed lost in a country soon to lose its way.

Derry blazed, policemen from all around the six counties were drafted in to quell the disturbances. My father and a number of the lads spent exhausting hours in Derry while the station at Forkhill was left essentially unguarded save for two young policemen, my mother, my brother and I, and my stick wielding grandmother.

They would come home in the early hours absolutely shattered. Bricks and the squalid life under which the nationalist community existed in Derry came flying over the cordons of police and smashed into the ranks leaving bloodied and frightened men.

It was all starting.

I have no wish to bore anyone with my personal feelings or opinions on the situation but the evening the Provisional IRA planted a bomb in Canary Wharf in London still brings a chill to my bones. Two more people lost their lives. And everybody blamed everybody else. Reminded me of a court case I once read about.

These two neighbours were always rowing. One would play his classical music too loud, the other refused to cut his trees which were encroaching on the neighbour's land and blocking out the sun. One day the classical music lover said he would turn his music down if his neighbour would cut his trees. He gave him three weeks to do it.

The neighbour agreed but in the following three weeks failed to keep to his side of the bargain. In a rage the classical music lover took a saw to the trees. There was hell to pay. After the court case at which the classical music lover was found guilty his wife said. "Why didn't you tell the judge that he said he would cut the trees? That it was his fault." The man looked at his wife.

"I didn't have to cut those trees down but I did it. I did it because I wanted to do it. I am responsible for what I do. Not you, not him, not God. But me."

Maybe if we Irish accept responsibility for what we do and stop blaming everyone else then we might, just might, have a chance.

And now we have new Ceasefires and the establishment of a Peace Agreement in an attempt to take us out of the dark ages. I am prompted by the memory of those whom I knew personally and who are no longer with us to have at least the hope of peace.

Sammy Gault: policeman, killed in the Enniskillen horror. Sammy never had a bigger smile on his face than when he was off on leave. Back to his beloved lakes of Fermanagh.

Big Willie Hunter: policeman, gunned down at Jonesborough in 1961. Big Willie was politeness itself. The night before his murder he called round to see my father to ask, without much confidence, was there anyway he could be relieved of 'doing the bags' (standing guard at the sandbagged entrance to the station). Willie had met this girl and wanted to take her to a dance. My father said no problem, he would sort something out. Willie went to the dance and my father 'did the bags'.

Thomas Morrow: policeman, killed by a bullet ricocheting off a factory wall at Camlough in 1972. In a few weeks time he was to marry his girlfriend.

Gerry 'Scullions' McKiernan: IRA man. Scullions shot himself outside a hotel just over the border, apparently overcome by remorse at what he had done or was about to do. In the twenty-a-side football games we used to play you would always want him playing on your team. He was like a freckled faced whirlwind. I always remember him with a big smile on his plump features.

Billy Turbitt: policeman. Billy was shot dead in an ambush at a crossroads between Crossmaglen and Camlough in 1978. The gunmen took his body away and chucked it in a river. He was found weeks later. Billy was one of the many mobilised men who passed through Forkhill and he would always say how grateful he was to my father for helping him prepare statements, and indeed my father would type up Billy's statements for him.

Raymond McCreesh: IRA man. One of the hunger strikers who died, died it's said without ever having a girlfriend. He used to do the milk run with my brother when they were younger. One time when the milkman was ill my brother drove the lorry with Raymsey as his passenger. Heading up a particularly muddy, cow pat adorned laneway, Raymsey shouted: "Go on, Leo, ye boy, keep her going." Words which splattered the air as the hole in the floor of the lorry treated both Leo and Raymsey to a splattering of cow dung.

Big George McCall: policeman. When he was stationed in Forkhill George owned a bit of land and would always prefer to be there during the day and then do the night shift. He was forever switching shifts without my father's knowledge so often that my father questioned who was running the station, him or the men? I don't think he got a reply. Big George was killed by one bullet in Newtownhamilton as he stood guard outside the barracks. He had swapped shifts.

These were all people I knew and at one time or other with whom I had a laugh. I remember others who joined the IRA. I remember them pointing toy guns at me down the Orney Lonen or in the rhododendron bushes behind the barracks. Some were imprisoned, others shot and wounded. They were all part of my life.

And my father.

How he and I suffered pain and enjoyed moments of air-punching jubilation over the years as we followed his hometown club, Coleraine, in their efforts in the Irish League. The player-manager then, the legendary bow-legged ex-Celtic and Irish international, the one and only Bertie Peacock. He also managed Northern Ireland and one day my father and I called into his pub in Coleraine for his autograph. He gave us both a drink and promised to get me the autographs of the Northern Irish team and those of their next opponents, Albania; as you can imagine, the latter were much sought after.

I got George Best's autograph; big Pat's; Johnny Crossan, himself an ex-Coleraine player; Jim McLaughlin; Bobby Irvine's and many others. I sold Best's years later for 2/6d (12 pence) to a girl I fancied. True love? Not at all, I had another autograph of his alongside those of the great Manchester United team of the late sixties.

What a great day we had at Windsor Park in 1965 when Coleraine beat Glenavon in the Irish Cup Final and a trip to Dalymount Park in 1969 saw us take Shamrock Rovers in the Blaxnit Cup (Bertie Peacock's last game). Having secured a 2-1 lead from the first leg watched by 20,000 at Windsor Park we fell behind in Dublin to two quick goals from Lawlor and O'Neill. Dessie Dickson, good old reliable Dessie, scored the winner for us amid scenes of elation. We won it again the next year. Maybe its time to reintroduce this North/South tournament.

I hated going to Mourneview Park for matches against Glenavon. We used to sit in what was loosely termed a stand (it was to a stand what miniature golf is to St Andrews) with a few Glenavon supporters. The most vociferous were a Lurgan trio of two men and one woman who berated the ref from start to finish and they were joined, from an opposing viewpoint, by my father who questioned the referee's every decision, even during half time. Dad, a man brought up on the idea that wingers wearing either the number seven or eleven shirt had to hug the touchline, was quick with his knowledgeable comments should either winger stray a yard or two infield. 'Stay out wide, out wide. What is he doing?' my father would moan. I wonder how he would cope with the marauding surges by the modern day full back?

My father didn't seem to notice I sat well away from him during the game and used to ease myself back towards him as the final whistle blew.

"Bloody referee," moaned my father.

"Bloody referee, a useless bastard," complained the Glenavon contingent. My father and the Glenavon trio never exchanged a word in all the years we went there. But then, was there a need? They were united, they might well have worn different scarves (actually, no – both Glenavon and Coleraine played in blue and white, Coleraine in stripes!) and the performance of the individual players was hardly ever criticised. Loyalty and all that. Now the referee, he was a whole different ball game. He was a bloody useless bastard.

How can I ever forget the day many years later when my father, mother, and my wife and I went to Craven Cottage to see Fulham play Hull. Fulham v Hull, not the match of a lifetime you might feel. George Best was playing for Fulham. As we walked to the stand to take our seats before the game the man himself came towards us on his way to the dressing rooms. I stood gawping. My all-time hero, the man whose photographs adorned the bedroom walls, the man who can rightly call himself 'God' if he wants to, was inches away. If the 'real' Gods wants to pop down and contest his claim, heh, we'll take it from there. My father spoke. "All the best, George" he said. Bestie winked shyly and raised his hand in what appeared a polite expression of gratitude. It made my father's day. Hell – it made his life.

My father saw big Willie Hunter die; he himself was ambushed in Jonesborough and shot eleven times in 1971 by two gunmen. When I arrived home that night having sank a few in a pub in Dundalk, where myself and my mate, Andy Weir, sang The Big Strong Man our house was surrounded with people. I immediately sobered up and went with my family to Daisy Hill Hospital to see my father as he lay with blood staining his mouth. Eleven bullets had hit him. During the attack he managed to jump out of the car and started to run but a bullet severed a nerve in his leg. He fell to the ground and dragged himself into the ditch. He tried to flag down two cars but they passed by. Finally a man stopped and took him to the hospital and physically carried him into casualty.

My father's life hung in the balance. Blood transfusions seeped through his body. We stood by his bed all night listening to his pain. In the morning the doctors thought it safe to move him to the Royal in Belfast. With the great care of the hospital staff, and I believe my father's love of life, he made it.

"They nearly shot the arse of me" he complained a few days later in hospital. Sandwich wrappers were found at the spot where they had fired from. They say you shouldn't drink on an empty stomach. But kill...

On 18 June 1982 as Northern Ireland were battling in the World Cup, the previous night we had drawn with, I think, Honduras, my father was shot dead. Dad was buried on Fathers Day. He wasn't to see us draw 2-2 with Austria and then beat Spain. I recently watched a video of that match, A Night In Valencia, when despite an obviously partisan crowd of over 50,000, a bent referee, and some outrageous tackling by the host nation, the 'wee six' manfully pulled together and beat Spain with a great goal by Gerry Armstrong. Jesus, what a night that must have been.

Sammy Mac; wee 'Dee' McCreery; Mal Donaghy, sent off for an innocuous challenge; big Billy Armstrong who supplied the cross for Gerry; all of them and more gave Northern Ireland a great night.

And I missed the game. My father would have loved it. We would have talked about it for years. That, and no doubt many other things. I was only just getting to know him as a friend. I liked it so far.

After dad had recovered from his injuries in 1971 he secured himself the post of Civilian Manager with the Crown Prosecution Service based in Newry police station; he took to it like a fish to water. He missed the police and the every day involvement but he enjoyed the crack with the lads and was forever starting debates/arguments and then slowly slipping away, leaving many at each other's throats.

Soon he adjusted to his new routine and my mum would pick him up for lunch and take him home after work each and every time from the same spot and at the same time. The day of his murder, my parents travelled home the usual route and as they turned in Balmoral Avenue, just off the Rathfriland Road, a car suddenly screeched in front of them. My father immediately recognising an attack shouted: "No, Winnie, no". The gunman leapt out of the car and fired a couple of shots through the windscreen, two missed, the third glanced off my mother's chest. Bruising over the next couple of days testament to how close she had come to her own death.

My father scrambled out of the car with a black umbrella in his hand to fight off the killers. My mother told me that she too was going to get out until she heard my father's voice (or what she thought was my father's voice, for even today she cannot confirm that he had spoken) telling her to stay where she was. The gunman fired into my father and he fell to the ground. The gunman stood over him and continued to fire bullets. My father was shot in the head, upper body and thigh. Within what seemed like seconds to my mother, the gunman and his accomplices were gone. My mother knelt beside my father and prayed for his soul as his eyes flickered. She gently closed them and caressed his bloodied face.

She will never forget the evil look on the gunman's face as he smiled.

Someone called Eamon Collins recently had a book published in which he describes his involvement in my father's murder and many others in the area. The book claims my father was targeted because he was in the RUC; he had medically retired eleven years by then. It is claimed the IRA couldn't tolerate a policeman living openly in Newry. The author claims that following my father and getting to know his movements was quite a determined surveillance operation because of the fact that my father regularly varied his routine and routes home. It is also claimed that my father once sat in his car in Dundalk outside an IRA safe house as my mother was away shopping. The IRA were going to shoot him there and then only they had difficulty finding a gun in this safe house. When I heard about this detail a vision entered my head of a bunch of IRA men running around a house looking for a gun. "You had it last," one might have uttered. "No, I saw you with it" could have been flustered comment from another.

If there was one thing my father hated was sitting in the car, he would have been out wandering the streets.

The author states my father was armed. He wasn't, he hated guns. The book also states my mother bent over my father and took a gun from him and chased the gunman with a gun in her hand. She apparently called the gunmen bastards as she tore up the road. Her life was apparently spared as the gunman considered her a brave woman.

We now call her Annie Oakley! As she said if she had had a gun she would have wiped out the whole street such was her aim.

The author claimed my father whimpered as he got out of the car to defend himself with a black umbrella. My mother remembers every second of the attack and will never forget the deathly silence splintered only by the life taking bullets.

I'll always remember the people who turned out for his funeral. Respect hung in the air. Policemen saluted his coffin as my brother and I carried him into the church. I felt so proud that I was his son. We carried him with strength. He was relying on us. Sean McCreesh from Forkhill took care of the funeral. Who else could we have asked? Many people came from South Armagh. I will also remember one of my aunt's on my father's side refusing to go into the chapel. Jesus Christ, even in death, bigotry comes to the surface. I suppose she was being even handed. She hadn't been inside a Protestant church in years.

I got the uneasy feeling that there are some of my relatives who wouldn't have bothered had my father died of a heart attack. They were able to say, their brother, brother-in-law, whatever, died as a victim of the troubles. It's almost a boast, one which I truly wish they were not able to make.

I thought, quite honestly, that his death would be the last. That the utter gut wrenching despairing grief that covered our family must somehow touch those responsible. Just a wee bit. How many families have thought the same since? We were so naive.

We can but hope that the Ceasefires and the Agreement last. So many people during the last cessation felt euphoric. I felt a deep re-emergence of grief. I missed my father like never before. I felt resentment. He should have been with the rest of us at least hoping for peace. I wanted him back knowing he should never have left. While the killing continued you accepted death as inevitable and in a way glad that he was in fact dead, so nobody could ever hurt him again.

I just wish that those who felt the uniform he once wore was unacceptable had looked beyond the clothing; my father was in fact in favour of a 'a nation once again.'

In his article the day after the Agreement was signed, Ross Benson, the Daily Mail journalist, spoke of the dramatic events and said "...if you listen hard you can hear the silent cheers of those innocents who lost their lives..."

Over three thousand died for Ulster or Ireland. I can but assume that the great majority would have declined the offer of dying for either. Had they been given the opportunity.

Take the guns out of Irish politics is an oft-mentioned cry. There should never have been any guns and I make this statement when I recall another episode in Forkhill not long before we left for Newry as my father had been promoted to Inspector and transferred there.

He and a constable colleague were out in front of the station sawing a few trees recently purchased for use in heating the station. The two policemen, their eye protected by goggles, fired up the saw, loaned by the Forestry people, and proceeded to create chunks of fuel, the noise of the saw intruding on the dominating hush which always seem to envelope the village. This took about an hour and during that time a constable would periodically shout at my father and wave him towards the station. My father, sweat blinding his eyes and possibly his common sense, indicated impatiently that he would be in in a few minutes. The exasperated constable told a senior constable of his unsuccessful efforts to get the sergeant into the station and the latter loaded a sub-machine gun and fired several shots out the back of the station into a grass bank. The wood cutting policemen fell to the ground, fearing an attack, and lay there for a few minutes until the senior constable came to the door. "Boss," he said in a relaxed manner, a yawn filing his features, the sub-machine gun cradled in his arms. "The District

Inspector wants you on the 'phone, he's been ringing for the past hour. Might be important."

"Why didn't you call..?" my father angrily began but on realising the situation walked past the constable and into the squad room. "You'll have to account for them bullets," was all he said to the constable. As to how they were accounted for is anybody's guess.

This story is a trip down memory lane for me. I hope it reminds some of the times which existed in South Armagh and introduces others to a South Armagh they probably think now could never possibly have existed. A time when RUC men would attend almost every social function, being fed and watered while the local kids looked after their landrover; when the very small Protestant population used the local Hibernian Hall to fund raise for their church and each and every Catholic attended; when the RUC would use the many unapproved roads which were known more intimately only to the smuggling fraternity, to dander into the south to buy cheaper drink and cigarettes; when many RUC men and their families were in tears, on the day of their transfer from the area, leaving 'their friends and neighbours' as they put it, and were never as happy again.

And when, as one policeman told me, the RUC were considered by the locals to be 'their police force'. I feel privileged to have experienced this unique time first hand. This was of course 'before the bandits' came. And there are those who will say they came in many different uniforms.

Author's Note

Eamon Collins was one of those responsible for bringing my father's life to a violent end. Collins, the one time reveller in murder and misery, was found by the roadside in January 1999, the victim of a terrible, gruesome attack. I felt nothing but shock and sadness at his death, the more so because of the appalling circumstances of this human being's last moments. His children must be in an awful state. No doubt there will be many people at a loss in understanding how I don't derive a degree of satisfaction or comfort, call it what you will, from the death of this man. I am unable to offer an explanation. It is however morally right and proper that I do not.

In Northern Ireland there is a tendency to categorise murder, thereby grading it as one which doesn't attract or deserve much sympathy, never mind revulsion. To their eternal shame there have been many over our tragic years who have done just that.